KNACK
MAKE IT EASY

ITALIAN
COOKING

KNACK

ITALIAN
COOKING

A Step-by-Step Guide to Authentic Dishes Made Easy

MARIA GRAZIA STRANIERI

Recipe variations by Linda Johnson Larsen

Photographs by Dana Devine O'Malley

Guilford, Connecticut
An imprint of Globe Pequot Press

Copyright © 2010 by Morris Book Publishing, LLC

Editor in Chief: Maureen Graney
Editors: Katie Benoit, Lara Asher
Edited by Linda Beaulieu
Cover Design: Paul Beatrice, Bret Kerr
Interior Design: Paul Beatrice
Cover Photos: Dana Devine O'Malley
Interior Photos: Dana Devine O'Malley

Library of Congress Cataloging-in-Publication Data is available on file.

ISBN 978-1-59921-778-9

Printed in China

10 9 8 7 6 5 4 3 2 1

Dedication

I dedicate this book to my handsome, strong, generous son, Sherwood, who was born from my heart and whose gentle, loyal heart gave me life in return. His constant encouragements and praise made writing this book a joy. "The pride I feel for you, my angel, is immense."

With love, always and forever,
Mamma

Photographer's Acknowledgments

Special thanks to food stylists Helen Jones and Sunny Nam, the location Pioneer Farm, mentor Dylan Cross, assistant foodie Julie Shiroishi, baby wrangler Sal Franca, loving supporter Mark O'Malley, food expert Marion Reinhardt, and the spirit of Hilda Schafer.

CONTENTS

INTRODUCTION

Respect for the land was taught to me by my grandmother at an early age. In the region of Calabria, Italy, where I lived with my mother, father, five siblings, and, of course my grandmother, the day would start early and the planning of the day's meals would be second only to the lighting of the *focolare,* or hearth, which served as the main source of household heat, both for cold winter days and chilly summer nights. By the time we returned home from school, the house would already be enveloped in wonderful aromas from the appetizing ingredients simmering on the stove, mixed with the soft voices of my mother and grandmother discussing the events of the day that had already taken place earlier in the morning, or, with just a hint of pride and satisfaction, how the neighbor's focaccia was not as good as theirs. Upon our entrance they would focus their attention immediately on us and the *merenda*—or snack—that would hold our hunger until dinner time. After having wolfed down our snacks, we would all compete for their attention, each of us convinced that the one screaming the loudest would receive the most notice.

After settling us with our homework, my mother and grandmother would return to planning the next fruit or vegetable canning of the season. Cooking with the seasons has always been the rule to Italian cooking and for good reason. In season fruit and vegetables have the best flavor and texture; as a result they require simple cooking to bring forth their full freshness, an advantage to busy and health conscious cooks. Since I can remember, and even before I was tall enough to reach a countertop, I was always trying to "help" in the kitchen, with my mother and grandmother gently directing me. I knew even then that I would never part with those exquisite aromas. Early on I was taught to recognize the change of the seasons by the colors of fruits and vegetables. As soon as autumn would make its

entrance, my grandmother and I would take long walks in the woods she owned, in search of mushrooms, instilling in me the serious, complicated way of choosing them. Mushrooms have an uncanny habit of springing up, maturing, and vanishing, within the space of a few days or a couple of weeks. Some types appear at the same spot year after year, others do not. Upon returning home my mother and grandmother would start the process of cleaning, storing, and preserving some, and cooking others. A good ragu of mushrooms consisted of a mixture of different types, each with its own distinctive taste, making it a highly flavorful dish.

Spring would announce its arrival with a gentle breeze that would make the curtains in open windows dance, while wonderful aromas of dinners made with freshly shelled peas and/or asparagus would waft through.

Summer in Calabria would arrive bouncing with the energy of a child let loose at the end on his last day of school. The sun is bright and dry, with temperatures usually reaching 90 degrees, perfect whether for lazy naps and long swims in the nearest pond. For supper, we would have large tomatoes, with sweet bright red pulp, sprinkled with the most sweet tasting basil; freshly roasted peppers, drizzled with the best extra virgin olive oil; chunks of Reggiano

ix

Parmigiano or Pecorino Romano; and bread with a crunchy crust and soft middle accompanied by the most delicious wine. After dinner, a *passeggiata* (walk) would be the perfect ending to a summer day. Friends would gather in groups in the "Piazza" enjoying each other's company and stopping at an outside café for espresso, cappuccino, or an *aperativo,* with the moon and stars shining bright in the background.

Winter is storytelling time. In winter, after dinner, we would all gather around the *focolare* and listen to stories told to us many times before, always with a different ending to keep the excitement alive. My *nonna* would roast chestnuts and dried figs on the fire, while we children would force ourselves to stay awake so as to not lose even a minute of it. Dinner would consist of robust dishes; prosciutto, salami of every variety, and black olives cured in olive oil are only a few of the dishes that were spread on the table, all accompanied by the hearty laughter of my family.

Food has always united families, friends, and people. Whether an elegant meal at the home of a friend or in one's own kitchen, Italian food brings memories of festivities, good times, and the wonderful mouth-watering flavors of delicious antipasti, pasta of every shape, crisp salads, fruits and vegetables straight from the garden, delicious sauces, fresh fish and seafood, high quality lamb, pork, and beef, freshly cut by the local butcher, baked goods like savory focaccia, and tirami su.

Italian cuisine has never been more popular, both in Italy where traditional recipes are enjoying some kind of rebirth, and other countries that no longer believe that Italian

food means cheap wines in wicker clad bottles, pizza, and spaghetti. Excellent chefs, retailers, and lots of representatives from Italy make sure that authentic products reach far beyond the country of origin. Almost everyone has a favorite Italian wine like Grignolino or Prosecco, and almost everyone recognizes Arborio rice as the base for a perfect risotto.

Italian cuisine is by all means not a single entity, but rather a vast variety in a country of relatively small size. From the Alps to the boot, Italy measures 750 miles plus two large Islands: Sicily and Sardinia. The changing geography of the peninsula gives each region a different climate resulting in a vast array of flavors and colors. A common tie for every province is the insistence on freshness, high quality, and the pride people take in the development of the products. Food in Italy is a daily celebration to be shared with family and friends, both at home and in the best restaurants. My hope is that the recipes in this book that I have chosen especially for you and your family will inspire you to establish joyful memories to last a lifetime.

SMALL TOOLS

A few small but essential tools in the kitchen can make cooking an experience to remember

Italian cooking doesn't generally require fancy gadgets. Italians prefer using their hands to feel the texture of the ingredients. However, there are a few things that every home chef needs to perform tasks to perfection. Modern technology continues to develop more specialized tools to reduce kitchen labor and expand the enjoyment of the cooking process. Hand tools are simple; all you need is some practice to develop good manual skills.

A good cooking utensil should distribute heat evenly; if it doesn't, it will develop hot spots that will likely burn the food before it is cooked. The thickness of the metal and the kind of metal on the pan affect the ability of the pan to cook evenly.

Bowls and More

- Stock deep bowls for making bread and pizza dough; use ovenproof high-sided bowls for baking fruits and pasta dishes.

- A colander is a perforated bowl used to drain washed or cooked vegetables, greens, pasta, and other foods.

- A strainer is a smaller version of a colander. It's cup-shaped, made of a screen mesh or perforated metal, and strains pasta and vegetables.

- A sieve is a screen of mesh supported in a round metal frame. Use it to sift flour and other dry ingredients.

Pizza Equipment

- A baker's peel is a long-handled wooden paddle for transferring pizza or bread to a hot baking stone or pan.

- A baking stone is a round stone placed in the bottom of the oven for baking bread and pizza. It helps the dough rise while it bakes, and gives it an even color and a crispy crust.

- While a stone is the best way to bake pizza, round perforated aluminum pizza pans will do nicely to create a crunchy crust.

A heavy pot cooks more evenly than one made of thin metal. Thickness is more important on the bottom. Different metals have different conductivity, which means they transfer heat at various rates. Aluminum is used for cooking utensils because of its ability to conduct heat and also because it's very light and therefore easier to carry around. However, aluminum is a relatively soft metal and should not be abused. It's not recommended for storing food or for long cooking of acidic foods, such as tomatoes, because it reacts chemically and discolors foods (sauces, for example), especially if they are stirred with a metal spoon or beaten with a metal whip.

Porcelain enamel-lined pots should not be used. These scratch and chip easily, thus giving bacteria a place to breed.

Nonstick plastic coated pans, such as Teflon, have a slippery finish that allows you to forgo cooking oil or butter. This makes cooking the low-fat way, which is increasing in popularity, much easier.

Peppermill

- A peppermill is an absolute necessity for Italian cooking, allowing you to grind up any type of fresh spices, like peppercorns.

- The peppermill comes in a variety of sizes and styles, so pick the one that you'll be most comfortable with.

- Keep the peppermill in a handy spot in your kitchen, because you will use it often.

Cheese Grater and Mill

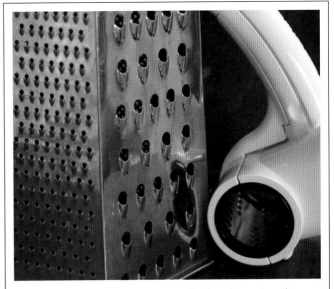

- The cheese grater is a four-sided metal box with different-size grids.

- It's used for shredding and grating cheese, vegetables, citrus rind, and other foods.

- Grating cheese in a cheese mill is a lot simpler; these grate hard cheeses faster, with no risk of injury.

- Good box graters are made of stainless steel, although rigid plastic provides a fine alternative.

UTENSILS

Your best friend in the kitchen is your knife; it requires only a little love

It's crucial to look at what type of metal a knife is made from. This metal must be able to hold a very fine edge. Carbon steel is everybody's favorite, but it discolors easily. Stainless steel will not rust, but it's hard to sharpen. High-carbon stainless steel, while a little more expensive, is the best way to go because it combines the best qualities of stainless steel and carbon steel: It won't rust, and it sharpens easily.

The chef's knife is still the most efficient tool for cutting, even better than a machine. It's faster and more precise and easier to clean. In order for your knife to perform at its best, you have to learn to keep it sharp and handle it correctly. A sharpening stone is the best way to sharpen your knives; an

Forks and Spoons

- Pasta forks are wooden or plastic tools specially shaped for lifting and stirring pasta.

- Tongs have a spring mechanism; use them to pick up and handle food.

- Use an assortment of wooden spoon sizes for a multitude of kitchen tasks.

- Other favorites are large stainless-steel spoons that hold about three ounces and are used for stirring, mixing, and serving.

Slotted Spoons

- Use slotted and perforated spoons when you need to separate liquid from solids.

- A skimmer is a perforated disk on a long handle.

- It's used for skimming froths from liquids and for removing solid pieces from soups, stocks, and other liquids.

electric sharpener will eventually consume their edges.

Hold the blade at 20-degree angle to the stone. Make light even strokes, the same number on both sides of the blade. Sharpen in one direction only, to obtain a regular even edge. Don't oversharpen. Wipe the knife clean.

A "steel" is not a knife, but an essential part of the knife kit. It's used not for sharpening an edge but rather to perfect the edge and keep the knife sharp during use. Follow these rules for using the steel:

Hold the blade at a constant 20-degree angle to the steel.

Make light strokes, first on one side of the blade and then on the other. Do not use more than five or six strokes on each side, as more than these will actually dull your knife.

If you use the steel regularly, you don't have to use the stone as often.

Sharp Knives

- A chef's knife has a wide blade 10 to 12 inches long and is used for slicing, chopping, and so on.

- Utility knives (6 to 8 inches long) and paring knives (2½ inches) have narrow, pointed blades and are used to cut and prepare fruit and vegetables.

- A slicer is a slender, flexible blade up to 14 inches long that slices and carves cooked meats.

- A boning knife has a thin pointed 6-inch blade; use it to separate meat and poultry from bones.

Specialty Utensils

- Among your specialty utensils, be sure to always keep on hand a vegetable peeler, a melon baller, a zester, scoops, and meat and instant-read thermometers.

- Another useful tool is the pastry wheel, a round rotating blade on a handle used for cutting rolled-out dough and pastry and baked pizza.

- A bench scraper or dough knife is a broad, stiff piece of metal with a wide wooden handle used to cut large pieces of dough and to scrape workbenches.

PASTA-SPECIFIC TOOLS

Regardless of whether you use fresh or dry pasta for dinner, some of the tools you need are the same

Pasta is the ideal food for entertaining. Whether you're hosting a large group of people or just a few friends, a well-made pasta dish will put a smile on everyone's face. This easy-to-prepare food is a blessing for the busy hostess, but more importantly it's fun.

It's unknown how long pasta has been a staple of our diet.

It appears to have been a popular dish in ancient Rome and Greece. As early as the third century B.C., Romans consumed something called "laganum" or "laganas," wide flat sheets of wheat-flour pasta. China had a noodle-like food as early as 3,000 B.C.; in the Arab world, couscous was popular.

In Italian, pasta means "paste," which is basically what it is:

Pasta Cooker

- A pasta cooker is a seven- or eight-quart stainless-steel three-piece set that includes two colander inserts, one small and one large, for draining pasta easily.

- Pasta cookers can be purchased in kitchen specialty stores, discount department stores, or almost anywhere kitchen equipment is sold.

Pasta Machine

- The pasta machine has rollers to thin out the pasta in preparation for cutting.

- These rollers produce ribbons of various widths and can be operated with a handcrank or an optional electric motor.

- There are many brands on the market; Atlas, Cross, and Mercato are all good.

a mixture of flour and water. That being said, however, pasta has a lot of nuances. Hard wheat semolina has a generous amount of glutens (proteins), which, when mixed with water, yield a stiff and elastic dough used to produce the many versions of dry pasta. Pasta made with this dough is firm and not mushy; it will remain this way throughout the cooking process, whether boiled or baked.

Many shapes of pasta are available today thanks to the invention of a specific machine called the extruder. When fitted with the right mold or dye, an extruder will transform dough into tubes, rigatoni, and much more.

Italian fresh pasta requires all-purpose flour and eggs to yield delicious golden noodles. At first glance, making fresh pasta may appear difficult, but with the right tools and a little practice the process can actually be simple and fun. Some of the fresh, flat noodles made with this dough include fettuccine and lasagna.

Attachments

- Pasta machines have several attachments you can buy separately. The motor allows for both hands to remain free and enables you to produce more evenly rolled sheets.

- Pass small pieces of dough one at a time through the rollers to produce extremely thin sheets of dough.

- The pasta machine comes with one ribbon cutter, which produces two shapes of pasta: fettuccine and linguine (fettuccine are about ⅛ inch wide; linguine, about 1/16 inch). Other ribbon cutters are optional.

Extra Tools

- When you're making fresh pasta, there are some extra tools you might want to have on hand.

- These include: a dough scraper, cookie cutters, kitchen towels, plastic wrap, a rolling pin, a pastry bag, a pastry cutter, and a chef's knife.

BIGGER TOOLS

When you use your equipment properly, the opportunities in Italian cooking are endless

Using your tools correctly in the kitchen is like having more than two hands to work with. Tools not only make our lives easier but also save us money.

Thanks to the tenderizer, you don't always have to buy the most expensive cuts of meat. The meat pounder can tenderize tougher but less expensive cuts of meat such as pork and veal.

The mixer and the blender also come in handy. Pasta dough, among other things, can be made in the mixer, saving on labor time. The blender is a must in the kitchen, not only for the obvious tasks, like mixing drinks, but also for creating the many sauces used in Italian dishes.

For your tools to work efficiently every time, you must clean

Mixer/Food Processor

- A food processor, or mini chop, will quickly slice, chop, and blend food together.

- Mixers are important and versatile tools for a variety of food mixing and processing jobs, both for baking and cooking.

Attachments

- There are three main mixing attachments: the wire whip, used for beating cream and eggs and making mayonnaise; the paddle, a flat blade used for general mixing; and the dough arm, used for mixing and kneading yeast dough.

- Make sure the bowl and

mixing attachment are firmly in place before turning on the machine.

- Turn off the machine before scraping the bowl or inserting a spoon or your hand into it.

- Turn off the machine before changing speeds.

and sanitize them on a regular basis. When working with bigger equipment, always keep food sanitation in the back of your mind. Bacteria lurk everywhere and can be drawn to dirty or unsanitized equipment. Keeping a tidy kitchen will help combat this.

Meat Pounder/Tenderizer

- The electronic meat tenderizer is run by motor. There are revolving rollers in the machine, which contains many small blades. These blades do the work of tenderizing meat.

- The hand-operated version functions similarly, minus the motor. Both versions can be easily disassembled for cleaning.

- The meat pounder is shaped like a hammer with one side smooth for pounding delicate cuts of meat. The other side, with teeth, is used for tougher cuts of meat.

Measuring Devices

- Measuring cups are available in 1-, ½ -, ⅓-, and ¼–cup sizes. They can be used for both dry and liquid measures.

- Measuring spoons are used for measuring very small volumes: 1 tablespoon, 1 teaspoon, ½ teaspoon, and ¼ teaspoon. They're used mostly for spices and seasonings.

- Ladles are used for measuring and portioning liquids. The size, in ounces, is stamped on the handle.

OVENS & RANGES

An Italian kitchen is never complete without a fully functioning oven

The oven and the range top are the two workhorses of the traditional kitchen, which is why the two are so often found in the same unit. Ovens are enclosed spaces in which food is heated, usually by hot air. In addition to baking and roasting, ovens can do a lot of the jobs usually done on the range. Many foods can be simmered, stewed, braised, and poached, thus freeing the stovetop for other tasks. A vast selection of ovens exists, most attached to a range.

Convection ovens, not to be confused with conventional ovens, are one of the fastest ways to cook. These ovens have fans that circulate and distribute air quickly and evenly. The temperature should be set 25° to 50°F lower than with a

Conventional Oven

- These ovens operate simply by heating in an enclosed space.

- They're most commonly found with a range attached.

Range Tops

- The range is still the most important piece of cooking equipment in the kitchen, even though some of its functions have been taken over by other tools, such as ovens.

- Range tops can come with open elements or burners

- (electric coils or gas flames) that heat quickly and can be turned off after use.

- Some ranges come with flat tops or hot tops. Here, burners are covered with steel plates, leaving more space available for cooking.

conventional oven. Cooking times need to be watched closely or food will dry out quickly.

Barbecue ovens are like conventional ovens but with a big difference: They surround the food with wood smoke while it cooks, thus giving it that special flavor. You do need to add wood, such as hickory, to these ovens. They have a special smoke-making element that gets hot enough to produce smoke but not to start a fire.

Many cooks also appreciate the grill, which creates charcoal flavor in meats when their fat drips into the heat source.

Convection Oven

- These ovens contain fans that circulate air to distribute the heat rapidly throughout the inside.

- Thanks to this forced air, food cooks more quickly at lower temperatures.

Broiler

- Broilers generate heat from above; food items are placed on a grate underneath the heat source.

- Food must be watched closely to avoid burning.

- You can adjust the broiling temperature by raising or lowering the grate that hold the food.

POTS & PANS

The right equipment will lead you to a better and healthier life

The success of any given dish relies heavily on the right equipment. We take for granted basic equipment, such as proper pots and pans, gas, ranges, ovens, and refrigerators, but the fact is that until recently these much-needed tools weren't readily available. Food cutters, mixers, and modern cooking tools that control heat easily and accurately make our everyday life a breeze. We can expect more of these sophisticated tools to come onto the market, thanks to research and technology.

Modern equipment has also made it possible for us to be more attentive to our health. For sautéing, for example, nonstick pans are more popular than ever; with these pans, there is no need to add extra oils or sprays. Cooking methods that require no added fat are also becoming very accepted:

Stockpots

- These large, deep, straight-sided pots are used for cooking pasta and simmering large quantities of liquids.

- It's wise to have several stockpots in your kitchen for times when you need to make several dishes at once.

Saucepots

- A saucepot is much like a stockpot only smaller, to make stirring easier. These pots are used for sauces and other liquids.

- A saucepan is similar to a small, light saucepot but with one long handle instead of two loop handles.

- It can have straight or slanted sides and is most often used for general range-top cooking.

Simmering, poaching, baking, and steaming are all healthier ways to prepare food.

The proper pot or pan can help cook foods at a faster rate, distribute heat evenly, and ensure that foods achieve high levels of flavor. A wide variety of pots and pans lets you make a wide variety of meals.

Sauté Pans

- A slope-sided sauté pan is also called a frying pan.

- It's used for general sautéing (frying gently) and frying of meats, fish, vegetables, and eggs.

- A straight-sided sauté pan is similar to a shallow, straight-sided saucepan except heavier.

- Use it for browning, sautéing, and frying. It can also be used for cooking sauces and other liquids when fast reduction is required.

Cast-Iron Skillets

- Cast iron makes for very heavy, thick-bottomed fry pans.

- They are used for pan-frying when very steady, even heat is desired.

- A brazier is a round, broad, shallow, heavy-duty pot with straight sides.

- It's used for browning and stewing meats.

11

OILS, WINES, & VINEGARS
Not all oils, wines, and vinegars are equal

Italian cuisine is not a single entity. From northern to southern Italy, taste in food, wine, olive oil, and customs are vastly different. Different climates produce different products. For example, each type of wine grape needs a specific kind of soil to grow.

Friuli-Venezia Giulia, a region of central Italy, offers elegant white wines, while the southern part of the same region is suitable for creating strong red wines. Some of these wines are among the best of Italy.

Vinegar has been used as a flavoring since ancient times. Romans used to take it as medicine. It's used in modern kitchens to flavor foods. With a splash of vinegar, bell peppers become more digestible, sauces become brighter, and oil-based dressings become tangy and delicious. Vinegars

Olive Oil

- There are four grades of olive oil. Extra-virgin is the highest grade and the most pure.

- It is made from the first press of the olive; its taste is very fruity and sweet. It is used for salads and drizzled over cooked food. It loses flavor when cooked.

- Regular olive oil is made from the second press of the olives. It's still fruity but less expensive and therefore used mostly for cooking.

White and Red Wines

- White, rosé, and sweet dessert wines should be served at colder temperatures than red wines.

- Do not serve a strong wine with a delicate meal, and vice versa.

- Don't worry about choosing white wines only for fish

- and red wines only for red meat. For example, you can serve a robust white wine like Greco with meats and a medium-bodied red wine such as Barbera with fish.

- See the resource section for more on wine.

flavored with herbs have become popular.

Vinegar does not necessarily have to be made from wine; honey and fruits are also used. The Egyptians were the first to make and use honey vinegar, which very well could be the oldest type known. Honey vinegar is used on salads, sauces, and sweet-and-sour dishes. Raspberry, cherry, and other fruit vinegars are best in salads and in sauces. Tarragon, bay, and rosemary vinegar are particularly good on fish and salads.

After Spain, Italy is the second largest producer of olive oil. Only the Lombardy and Piedmont regions of Italy offer climates that are unsuitable for olive growing; every other Italian region produces olives of different sizes and colors that yield a variety of flavors. Liguria gives us a delicate olive oil; Tuscany delivers a tangy one; and Apulia produces a sharp and fruity type.

Balsamic Vinegar

- Genuine balsamic vinegar is at least fifty years old, sweet in taste, and used very sparingly because of its high price. It is often used on desserts or other delicacies.

- While regular vinegar is made from leftover wines, balsamic is made with the best grapes available, just like the best wines, and the process is equally labored.

- For ordinary use, buy regular balsamic vinegar which is rich in flavor, not too acidic, not too sweet.

Other Specialty Oils

- Olive oil can be infused with the ingredients that you like most.

- These oils are mostly used for salads or to dunk good crusty breads in.

- The best ingredients with which to infuse extra-virgin oil are fresh herbs and garlic. Start with any fresh herbs, such as a bunch of fresh oregano and five or six big cloves of garlic cut in half. Place these in a wine-size bottle; fill it with extra-virgin olive oil. Let the mixture marinate for a week in the refrigerator before using.

13

HERBS

Herbs make for flavorful, low-fat alternatives to oils when cooking

Herbs have been around forever. The ancient Romans and Greeks, for example, knew which herbs to use for healing and which for cooking. However, it wasn't until the Renaissance that the full importance of various herbs in culinary and medicinal practices was rediscovered.

The first Italian cities to cultivate aromatic gardens were Pisa and Padova (Padua), followed by Florence, Lucca, and Siena.

Parsley was considered a tonic that helped alleviate kidney stress; tarragon helped people recover from snake bites; basil cured stomachaches and nausea; thyme cured hangover headaches; fennel soothed children; rosemary was a tonic for the nerves; peppermint was a stimulant; and so on.

Today the healing powers of herbs are debatable, but it is very difficult to argue their importance in cooking. Italy is

Dried Herbs

- Marjoram can be used with thyme. The delicate flavor of fresh, sweet marjoram is easily lost in slow cooking, so add it at the end.

- Thyme goes well with vegetables, fish, and stews. It blends easily with garlic, onion, brandy, or red wine in cooking. It's great in

marinades for pork or game.

- Oregano provides the pungent flavoring of pizza. It goes well with onions, eggplant, tomatoes, beans, and meat. Add it fifteen minutes before the end of the cooking or it will be too overpowering.

Fresh Herbs

- Basil, sage, rosemary, bay leaves, parsley, and marjoram should all be kept fresh, if possible.

- Fresh basil goes well with tomatoes, eggplant, bell peppers, and cooked dishes, among others. As pesto, it makes the ultimate pasta sauce.

- Sage nicely accompanies ham, liver, sausages, and veal, and adds flavor to beans, kebabs, and peas.

- European cooks add parsley almost as easily as salt. Always used fresh, it is essential to many sauces (often together with lemon) and a number of butters.

prolific in the growth of herbs. Many residents also grow a few herbs in wooden boxes and on balconies and windows. In southern Italy fennel grows wild on the side of the road. Leaves, seeds, stems, and bulbs are used for cooking and are especially good with pork. Mint is often used in Tuscany; its leaves flavor mushrooms, salads, vegetable dishes, and various herb liqueurs.

If you cannot find fresh herbs, you can use dried ones, but use them very sparingly because dried herbs have a concentrated flavor. Rosemary and oregano retain their flavor very well when dried but do not keep their aroma indefinitely; about a year is the maximum shelf life of such herbs. Rosemary is normally used whole, in bunches, because individual leaves are hard and not very pleasant to chew. It's easer to remove from cooked food if used in whole sprigs.

Herb Staples

- Plan on having the following herb staples in your pantry or spice rack: marjoram, parsley, rosemary, bay leaves, sage, basil, oregano, thyme, and garlic.

- Bay leaves are used fresh or dried. They are basic to Italian and French cooking in marinades, stews, pickles.

- Fresh marjoram, chopped, with lemon juice, salt, and black paper, makes a very good dressing.

Specialty Herbs

- Powdered saffron gives the most flavor, but it's more readily available in strands.

- Finely chop saffron before using. It's expensive and is used mostly in risotto.

- Mint is an aromatic herb. Its leaves are added to mushroom dishes, and also used in many salads and vegetable dishes.

15

TOMATOES & TOPPINGS

The pomodoro (gold apple) is one of the juiciest fruits available—but usually served as a vegetable

The tomato is actually a fruit, although we eat it like a vegetable (this text refers to it as a vegetable). It's Italy's preferred vegetable, eaten every day and with everything. There are thousand of varieties in the world. Technology is on the verge of developing new hybrid tomatoes that will be more disease-resistant and quicker growing. San Marzano tomatoes are used for canning and drying; their flesh is sweet and firm. Tomatoes on the vine (ramato) take their name because they grow in groups on the vine (rami). They are easy to peel and versatile in the kitchen.

Marena tomatoes, like every other tomato from southern Italy, are deliciously sweet, ripe, and red. The palla di fuoco, or

Canned Tomatoes

- When selecting canned tomatoes, always use whole peeled tomatoes that are firm and sweet smelling without being salty.

- The best tomatoes for canning are the San Marzano variety.

Tomato Paste

- Tomato paste (*conserva* in Italian) is usually used to thicken tomato and other sauces.

- Tomato paste is a good staple to have on hand in the kitchen. It tends to pop up a lot in Italian recipes.

fireball tomato, is popular in the north; it makes great mixed salad. Southern Italy exports tomatoes not only to northern Italy, but also all over the world. It's now the world's biggest supplier of high-quality tomato preserves. Canned tomatoes from southern Italy are a favorite because the flavor is sweeter and stronger than that of tomatoes outside Italy.

Another tomato product that sells very well, in or out of Italy, is tomato paste in various concentrations. It's made from dried tomatoes and concentrated into paste. Double concentrate is the best. Tubes are the most convenient packaging because they can be easily resealed. Use paste a tablespoon at a time; its full thickness can be detected only after it cooks in sauces, five minutes or more. Italy also features a third tomato product called *passata di pomodoro,* also known as tomato puree, which is thicker than tomato juice and contains more liquid than tomato paste.

Capers

- Capers are seeds of the caper bush that are available in jars with salt or wine vinegar.

- Refrigerate capers after opening.

- Capers can be used for salads, sauces, and fish.

Anchovies

- Anchovies are little Mediterranean fish that are preserved in olive oil and salt.

- Anchovies in oil are delicious on slices of fresh tomatoes with good, crusty bread and some chunks of Parmigiano Reggiano cheese.

- Anchovies make an especially nice treat accompanied by a glass of medium-bodied wine, either white or red.

CHEESE

Mozarella, Pecorino Romano, and Parmigiano Reggiano all add rich flavor to traditional Italian dishes

Like France, Italy operates a system of regulations to protect certain cheeses (and wines) under the acronym DOC (Denomination Controlled Origin).

Pecorino is the generic name for cheeses made from pure sheep's milk. The smooth, hard rind ranges from pale straw to dark brown in color. Each is characteristic of a specific area and a particular breed of sheep. For centuries, Pecorino Romano was made in the countryside around Rome, and it remains virtually unchanged to this day.

Parmigiano Reggiano's aroma is sweet and fruity; it's pale yellow in color, and the taste is fruity (like fresh pineapple), strong, and rich but never overpowering. It will keep in the

Formaggio

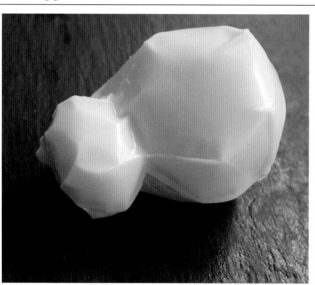

- Italy relies on the DOC (Denomination Controlled Origin) to protect the authenticity of its cheeses.

- In 1955 the Ministry of Agriculture and a consortium of cheesemakers agreed that cheeses with this stamp of approval could be made only in a specific region.

- Identifying and promoting specific cheeses this way helps to protect them from been copied while guaranteeing the consumer high quality.

Pecorino Romano

- Regions: Lazio and Sardinia

- Type: Hard cheese

- Source: Sheep's milk

- Culinary use: Table cheese, grating

- Stamp: DOC

- Pecorino is the generic name for cheeses made from pure sheep's milk. The smooth, hard rind ranges from pale straw to dark brown in color.

- Each is characteristic of a specific area and a particular breed of sheep.

refrigerator for months; it can also be frozen, and even grated when still frozen. The cows whose milk goes into the cheese are only allowed to eat fresh grass, alfalfa, and hay; this process guarantees the quality and the flavor of the cheese but drives the price for it higher.

Genuine mozzarella is made from the milk of the black water buffalo. It is usually sold as a snow-white ball, but also sometimes gently smoked. Fresh mozzarella is extremely perishable. It's at its best when eaten on the day it was made. Until modern food technology made possible the process of preservation, mozzarella was only a regional pleasure. It would be hard to imagine pizza without deliciously soft-melted mozzarella. As a result of the huge demand for this fresh, soft cheese, it is now also made with cow's milk. Strictly speaking, in this case it should not be called mozzarella but *fior di latte* (milk flower).

Parmigiano Reggiano

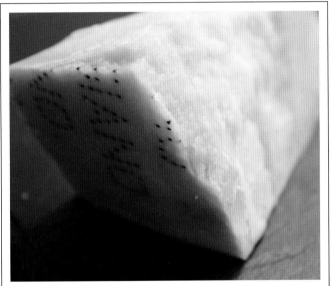

- Regions: Modena, Parma, Reggio Emilia, Bologna, Mantua

- Type: Traditional, unpasteurized hard cheese

- Source: Cow's milk

- Culinary use: Table cheese, grating in sauces and salads, served over pasta and risotto

- Stamp: DOC

- The aroma of Parmigiano Reggiano is sweet and fruity. This cheese will keep in the refrigerator for several months; it can also be kept and grated frozen.

Mozzarella

- Region: Campania

- Type: Semi-soft

- Source: Milk of the black water buffalo.

- Culinary use: Often served with fresh tomatos in a salad as well as on pizza.

Also used in many classic pasta dishes and as the Parmesan topping to popular meat and chicken entrees.

- Stamp: DOC

- Mozzarella is shiny porcelain white with a sweet perfume.

DOUGH

Pasta can easily be transformed into something extra special by infusing paste or spinach into the dough

Many people make different dough for each bread product, but after baking more than my share, I realized that this is not necessary. One classic dough recipe will suffice for breads, pizza, pasta, and many more dishes.

Ingredients for basic dough:

1 tablespoon active dry yeast (1 package)

1¾ cups warm water, divided
1 teaspoon salt
4–5 cups unbleached all-purpose flour
Extra-virgin olive oil

In a large bowl, dissolve the yeast in ¼ cup of the warm water. Let the yeast rest in the water for about 10 minutes.

Yeast

- Mixing yeast dough has three main goals:

- To combine all the ingredients into a uniform, smooth dough.

- To distribute the yeast evenly throughout the dough.

- To develop gluten (proteins) so breads products will rise and won't be heavy.

Flour

- Flour is made of cereal grain. It is the main ingredient for bread, pasta, and pastries. Wheat flour is the most common.

- *Durum wheat* flour is high in gluten (the stuff that makes dough elastic). It's used mostly for bread and pizza.

- All-purpose flour is blended wheat flour, used for most household baking needs.

- Semolina flour, coarse-ground flour mixed with unbleached flour, yields perfect dry pasta and breads. It's best to use a machine with this dough—it's very hard to work with by hand.

Add the remaining 1½ cups water and the salt. Add the flour 1 cup at a time; you might not need to add all of it. Work the mixture until it's no longer sticky and can be formed into a ball. Place the dough on a floured work surface and knead it for 5 to 10 minutes, until it is shiny and elastic.

Grease a bowl with olive oil (generously) and put the dough in it; turn the dough a few times to make sure all the sides are coated with oil. Cover the bowl tightly with plastic wrap. Let the dough proof (rise) for 4 hours until it doubles in size. Punch the dough down, transfer it to a floured surface, and

work it a few more times. Proceed with your recipe.

You can make as many batches of this dough as you wish. You can double, triple, or even quadruple your ingredients and make lots of individual batches, use one and freeze the rest, individually, for later use.

Eggs

- The egg yolk is high in both fat and protein and contains iron and many vitamins. Its color ranges from light to dark yellow, depending on the diet of the chicken.

- AA is the best and freshest grade of eggs; when broken onto a flat surface, a grade AA egg will not spread around. Grade A- is for hard-boiled eggs (grade AA eggs are difficult to peel). Grade B- is good for baking.

- Eggs keep for weeks if stored in the refrigerator at 36˚F.

Salt

- Salt plays an important role in baking. It helps make dough more stretchable, improving the texture of breads.

- Salt keeps dough from rising too much, preventing wild yeasts from interfering with the quality of bread products.

- There is some debate over which salt is best to use in cooking: sea salt, which is pure and has more minerals than regular salt, or kosher salt, which is human-made and more delicate. Both are fine.

21

EXTRAS

Not only are olives, nuts, and truffles good pantry staples, they also make terrific appetizers

Harvesting olives for oil is not the only way to enjoy them. Since ancient times, Romans have used olives as an appetizer and to clear the palate at the end of an elegant meal. A vast selection can be found in any supermarket or specialty food store. The ones with pits are tastier, as pits have lots of flavor. Keep olives in a constant marinade; just take the pits out before serving. Olives are best when bought loose from the case, not in cans or jars, and they are kept constantly in brine, which keeps them juicy and flavorful.

Nuts are an ideal source of nutrients, including vitamin E, and are rich in protein and dietary fiber. Even though they're high in fat, this is good fat. To reap the benefits, you only need

Olives

- A wide variety of olives can easily be found in any supermarket.

- Fresh ones (in the dairy section) are the best; try them all and decide on your favorite.

- Harvesting olives for olive oil is not the only way to enjoy them.

- Use them in salads, appetizers, on pizza, and breads.

Nuts

- Nuts are an ideal source of nutrients. They are high in fat but good for growth, healthy skin, and hair, among other things.

- Almonds are good for the skin, bones, and heart.

- Cashew nuts are good for bones.

- Walnuts help prevent heart disease.

a handful. They are necessary for growth, healthy skin, and shiny hair, among others things. They are used in salads, in pasta, and to garnish vegetable dishes. Nuts can be ground coarsely and used to coat pieces of chicken and fish.

Truffles—a type of mushroom—are very hard to find and in great demand. They're very expensive. While common mushrooms grow above the ground and in abundance, truffles grow under the soil. Pigs and dogs, with their strong sense of smell, are used to sniff them out. White truffles are found in Tuscany and Piedmont; black ones, in Umbria. They're more versatile than the white kind, for they can be added to sauces for flavor as well as eaten raw.

Mushroom season begins with the first rain in October. To dry mushrooms for use in the off season, spread them in the cellar or a dark, dry place on top of a clean sheet, and leave them until they are dried. Then store them in jars.

Truffles

- White truffles should always be eaten raw.

- Never boil black truffles; just heat them gently. Black truffles are eaten raw but can also be used to flavor other dishes.

- Only use truffles for dishes that do not have their own strong flavor.

Dried Mushrooms

- Dried mushrooms can be substituted for fresh.

- It takes around seven or eight pounds of fresh mushrooms to make a pound of the dried kind, so fewer are required for the same recipe.

- Soak dried mushrooms in warm water for thirty to forty minutes, squeeze out any excess water, and cook as usual.

- The liquid from the mushrooms can be used to flavor other dishes.

ESSENTIALS
Would pizza really be the treat we love without garlic, onions, and basil?

I wish everybody knew the taste of fresh garlic (also called green garlic)—regular garlic picked before it's fully grown. It's available for only a few weeks a year, between May and June, and can be found at farmer's markets. Fresh garlic looks like a big scallion and can be eaten raw or cooked. Its taste is much gentler than the fully grown variety. Mature garlic is easier

to peel if the cloves are bigger. Avoid elephant garlic; even though it belongs to the same family as garlic, it does not possess the same qualities.

Caramelized onions are a savory treat. I use them in panini; I add some chunky pieces of Parmigiano Reggiano, wrap them in aluminum foil, and bake in a 400°F oven for approximately

Garlic

- Raw garlic has a strong taste; when cooked, however, it is mild and leaves no trace on the breath.

- When you sauté garlic, remove it from the pan before it gets brown.

- Garlic blends well with almost everything: meats, vegetables, herbs, and spices.

- Be sure to buy hard cloves that have no spots.

Onions

- Red onions are very mild and are used mostly for salads.

- White onions are used in soups, in sauces, and for frying.

- These are milder than the more popular variety, the yellow onion.

15 minutes. The onions make all the difference! Caramelized onions freeze well; make a lot so you can save yourself extra tears. Storing onions in a paper bag in the crisper drawer in the refrigerator may help stop the tears later on when they're cut. Others say that lighting a candle while cutting also helps.

Basil has a spicy flavor and scent. This herb is best when fresh but will keep in a jar with olive oil and a little salt. Combined with garlic, it gives a peppery flavor to plain chicken dishes. As pesto, it makes the best sauce ever.

Lemons are available year-round and around the world. Lemon juice is tangy and fresh and brings out the taste of whatever food it's paired with. Whether you cook with lemons, flavor your tea with them, or roast them, life is more fun with lemons in it.

Basil

Lemons

- This herb has a spicy flavor and scent. It's best when fresh but will keep in a jar with olive oil and a little salt.

- Fresh basil goes well with tomatoes (raw and cooked), eggplant, and bell peppers.

- Basil also goes great with firm fish, such as sea bass.

- Lemons have a tangy, tart flavor and fresh citrus scent. They should be stored in the refrigerator and then taken out and warmed to room temperature before use.

- They are perfect to liven up salads and salad dressings, sauces, fish, and even vanilla ice cream. (The average lemon has about three tablespoons of juice.)

- Use slices to cook fish and use the peel to flavor espresso. Lemon juice also helps to neutralize the odor of fish.

VEGETABLES

Spring vegetables add fresh flavor and color to any simple meal

Vegetables are very important in Italian cooking. There are three stages to peppers: Green is the first stage of maturity, red the second, and yellow the final. With each of the stages, the pepper becomes sweeter.

To fry assorted peppers, place a large Teflon frying pan over medium-high heat on the stove. Add 3 to 4 tablespoons olive oil and let the oil warm up. Take the seeds out of 10 assorted peppers and cut them into strips. Add the green variety first; fry them, stirring continually, for 5 to 6 minutes. Next, add the red peppers. Turn the heat to medium and sauté, uncovered, for 5 minutes. Finally, add the yellow peppers and keep sautéing for 3 to 4 minutes longer. Stir constantly, and add salt and black pepper to taste. Serve the peppers as a side dish with pork chops and refrigerate leftovers to use later in

Sweet Peppers

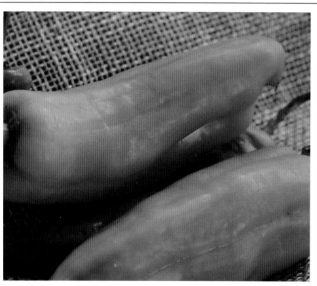

- Red and yellow peppers are more expensive than green because of the extra care they require to reach maturity.

- Try all three colors together, fried. Start frying the green variety first because they take the longest to cook. Then add the red, then the yellow.

- For the best flavor, add 6 or 7 leaves of fresh basil to the last minutes of the cooking process.

Hot Peppers

- Peperoncini, also known as chile peppers, paprika, or Spanish peppers, come in various sizes.

- When experimenting at home, be cautious: Use too little at first rather than too much. The spiciness of peperoncini increases when they're cooked.

a panini. Fried peppers always taste better if left in the refrigerator overnight.

Another Italian staple, peperoncini (also known as chile peppers, paprika, or Spanish peppers), come in various sizes. Small peppers are the hottest, although the long ones are hot as well.

In southern Italy ripe plum tomatoes are dried in the Mediterranean sun until they're ready to be packed in olive oil or made into tomato paste. They can be found in any supermarket in jars with or without oil.

The most common eggplant, the globe eggplant, is available year-round. Different varieties are available at farmer's markets from mid- to late summer. The smaller the eggplant, the tastier it is. The flesh should be shiny and taut. Globe eggplant needs to be salted to get rid of the bitterness.

Tomatoes

- The tomato has to be the favorite vegetable for Italians and is served on a daily basis, all year round, in one way or other.

- Tomatoes can be found in pasta, salads, or stuffed, among other dishes.

- There are many shapes and flavors, depending on the region's soil.

Eggplant

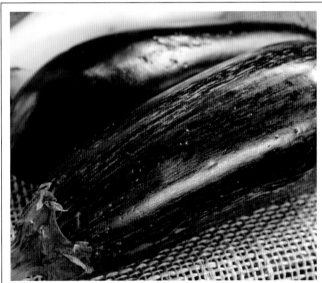

- Eggplants come in different colors (purple, white, green) and sizes. They can have a bitter taste when raw but become tender and flavorful when cooked.

- They can be used in tapenades as an appetizer and are often found in traditional Italian dishes, such as Eggplant Parmesan or Eggplant Rollatini.

- A wide variety of eggplants are available in the summer. Eggplants can be roasted, grilled, or baked—or even stuffed.

FRUIT

Italians like to enjoy sweet, refreshing, and juicy fruits all year round

Fruit is an important part of the Italian diet. Melons are grown all over central and southern Italy. They were first grown in Asia and Africa and eventually made their way to Italy. Honeydew has a white, pale yellow, orange, or pale green flesh; the outer skin is yellow or green. Some melons are bigger in size with green skin and bright red flesh with lots of seeds. The redder the flesh, the sweeter the taste.

Grapes are perhaps Italy's most famous fruit. Italy's soil is ideal to grow grapes, not only for winemaking, but also for exceptionally good desserts. In the region of Apulia, grapes are especially sweet and juicy because of the fertile soil and the warm climate. They are in great demand throughout Italy and Europe. Grapes in Italy are frequently served with other fruits as dessert at the end of a meal.

Melons

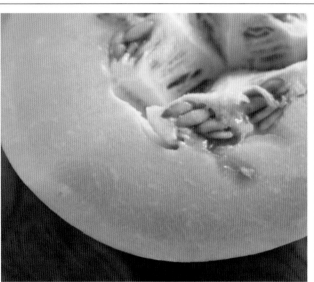

- Melons are grown all over central and southern Italy. Here are a few tests to help check to see if the fruit is ripe:

- Pressing: The stem end should feel softer than the rest of the melon.

- Tapping: If you gently rap the fruit with your knuckles, it should sound full rather than hollow.

- Weight: Ripe melons are heavy; avoid any light-weight melons.

- Smell: The fruit should smell appetizing and sweet, with no hint of decay.

Oranges and Citrus Fruits

- Taracco: Blood oranges are very popular.

- Biondo commune: The common blonde is one of Sicily's most popular oranges.

- Ovale: Compact, juicy, and good for storing.

- Comune: A common type of mandarin.

- Tardivo Ciacculli (late): Another type of mandarin in Sicily.

- Lemons: Femminello (little feminine), Verdello (little green), and Monachello (little monk) have different origins and shapes.

At the end of a meal, sliced pears are served baked, drizzled with a liqueur of your choice, and topped with thin slices of Parmigiano Reggiano. This dish also makes a healthy afternoon snack.

The Italian term for prickly pears or Indian figs is *fichi d'India*. Many varieties are grown all over Italy, yielding different tastes.

Lemons and oranges originated in Sicily in the twelfth century. They were both originally bitter fruits. Five hundred years later monks planted sweet lemon and orange plants and realized that the soil of Palermo, Sicily, was perfect for growing these delicious fruits. Mandarins, grapefruits, and clementines came much later. Sicily's reputation for producing the best citrus fruits remains unchallenged.

Grapes

- Italy is a land of grapes.

- Italy grows grapes not only to make wine but also to serve for dessert, often with other fruits.

- The green and golden grapes are used in fruit salads.

Pears and Prickly Pears

- Fruit is traditionally served as refreshing dessert at the end of a meal. Pears and peaches are also served stuffed and baked.

- The Italian term for prickly pears or Indian figs is fichi d'India. They hail from the cactus family and are a bright fuscia color.

- Prickly pears must be peeled to remove the small spines on the outer skin before eating. Stripped of their prickly skin, the delicate fruit is served sliced and drenched in dry Marsala.

GRAINS

Italian cooking would not be complete without a wide variety of grains

In addition to rice and wheat, corn is one of the three most important grain crops in the world. Most of the world's production occurs in the Midwest and Plains states of the United States. Corn flour, or cornmeal, is flour from corn, ground coarsely, from which we make polenta. Sweet corn is mistakenly considered a vegetable and not a grain because it's

eaten fresh like a vegetable. Popcorn is a different kind of corn that contains moisture, which causes the kernels to explode when they're heated because the steam can't escape.

Whole wheat flour is made by grinding the entire wheat kernel. White wheat flour is milled from wheat kernels after the outer skin, called bran, has been removed along with the

Rice

- Recipes for Italian rice dishes call for various types with different consistencies and cooking qualities.

- Household rice has small, round grains and cooks in 13 or 14 minutes, getting very soft. It's used for desserts and soups.

- Superfine rice, such as Arborio, has long, thick grains suitable for risotto. It takes 18 minutes to cook.

- Standard rice has long, shaped grains. It takes 16 minutes to cook, remains firm, and is suitable for risotto and rice salads.

Corn

- In addition to rice and wheat, corn is one of the three most important grain crops in the world.

- It is often used in Italian dishes.

- Polenta, for example, is made of cornmeal.

germ. Wheat flour contains a specific protein called gluten, which is one of the most important ingredients in baking. Glutens make bread rise and also prevent it from being heavy.

Flour comes in different types depending on how much gluten each contains. Flour with large quantities of gluten is called "strong." Bread flour (semolina) is a strong flour used to make breads. Conversely, flours with fewer glutens are called "weak" flours. Cake flour is a weak flour made from soft wheat. It is smooth in texture and white in color and is used for pastries.

All-purpose flour falls between the two—it's weaker than bread flour but stronger than cake flour. It is used for both breads and pastries. Buckwheat is considered a cereal grain because it's produced and processed in the same way as grains. Buckwheat is actually an herb native to Russia. It doesn't need topsoil to grow. The harvest is available twice a year. Buckwheat has a hearty, grassy flavor with a slight taste of cocoa; it's even better when toasted.

Semolina

- Semolina is created by grinding and sifting grain into a powdered form that varies in texture from soft to coarse.
- It's used for making breads, cakes, pastries, and many other baked goods.

Wheat

- There are more than 360 varieties of wheat throughout the world.
- Durum wheat used for breads, while semolina is used for pasta.
- These are only two examples of the wide variety of wheat.

31

ROLLING OUT FRESH PASTA

Whether you roll your fresh pasta by hand or with a machine, always have fun with it

The five steps of the pasta-making process are: mixing, resting, rolling, cutting, and drying.

Learning to roll your own fresh pasta is a must for Italian chefs. Hand rolling produces more desirable pasta. When you roll by hand, the dough is stretched rather than compressed. This creates more porous pasta that absorbs sauce better.

Practice a few times on dough you don't mind discarding until you feel confident you have it right. You can follow the directions below.

If you'll be using a machine, cut the dough into chunks the size of golf balls and cover. Set the smooth rollers in your machine to their widest setting. Flour them and start

Ingredients and Tools:

Dough

Work surface

Rolling pin

Rolling Pasta: Step 1

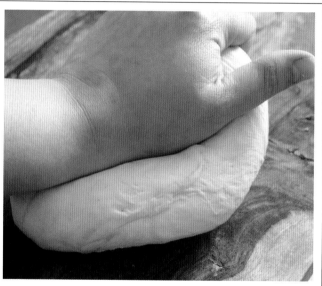

- Remove the dough from the plastic wrap. Knead it for 1 minute so the moisture that has collected on the surface is worked back into the dough. Flatten the dough slightly with your hands to form a round disk; place it on the work surface.

- Roll the dough away from

you with the rolling pin from two-thirds of the way down the disk. Stop just before the top edge.

- Turn the disk 90 degrees and repeat. Continue until the dough is ¼ inch thick.

- Roll the edges of the dough onto the pin.

running the dough through the rollers, one piece at a time. Repeat. Each piece should be run through the rollers four times. Cover the sheets with plastic wrap, separating them with paper towels.

Adjust the rollers to the second widest setting, flour them, and run each sheet through once, lengthwise, without folding. Repeat the rolling process once at each progressively narrower setting of the pasta machine until you've gone through all of the settings. Hold the sheet with one hand while passing it through the machine and use the other hand to catch the sheet. The sheets of dough should retain a uniform width and get longer with each pass through the machine. Stop the machine periodically to cut and slide the most recently rolled portion out flat onto the work surface. Do not let the rolled dough bunch up as it comes out of the machine. The finished sheets of dough should be paper-thin and 14 to 18 inches long. Flour, stack, and cover the sheets with paper towels; let them rest for 20 minutes.

Rolling Pasta: Step 2

- Hold the dough at the bottom of the disk while you gently stretch and roll it onto the pin.

- Turn the dough on the pin 90 degrees; unroll. Repeat five times.

- Roll the dough snugly back onto the pin from the top. As you roll the pin back and forth, slide your hands together and apart to trace the shape of a W.

- When the dough is rolled up, turn it with the pin, unroll, and repeat.

Rolling Pasta: Step 3

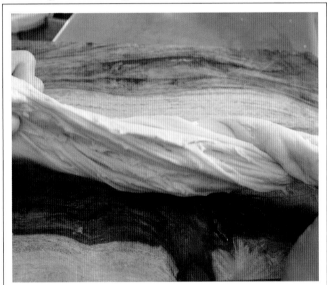

- Continue stretching the dough until it's transparent, letting it drape over the edge of the worktop.

- Lay the dough sheet on a kitchen towel to dry.

- Only the palm of your hands should contact the dough on the rolling pin.

- To stretch rather than compress the dough, do not push down on it but rather out and away from you.

INGREDIENTS

CUTTING FRESH PASTA
The number of fresh pasta shapes is endless

Before cutting pasta, the sheets you just rolled must dry until they feel leathery. This is so that the pasta won't stick to itself, and doesn't dry out so much that it becomes too brittle to cut. Some shapes need to be cut by hand, which is easy and requires just a little practice. Hand-rolled pasta must be hand-cut. If you do not intend to cook the pasta within a few hours, then you must store it either in the refrigerator or in the freezer.

One of the most interesting things you can do with sheets of dough is to cut them into squares, circles, or rectangles, stuff them with succulent filling, and fold them just like little sacks. To close them, just gather and pinch the edges tight.

Ingredients and Tools:

Pasta of your choice

Large sharp knife

Fluted pastry cutter

Tagliatelle

- Tagliatelle: ⅕ inch

- Tagliatelle: ⅓ inch

- To make tagliatelle, loosely roll up the sheet of pasta dough into a flat roll, about 2 inches across.

- Take a large knife and rest the flat of the blade against your knuckles. Cut the roll of pasta into ribbons of the desired width by moving your knuckles back along the roll after every cut. Unravel the ribbons.

Dough can be shaped in any way you desire; you can be creative without even using any tools. Make it a family event, involve the children, and teach them early in life how fun cooking can be. Stuffed shells are always everyone's favorite. They can be filled with almost anything. Try making new stuffings with eggplant, sun-dried tomatoes, prosciutto, or lobster. Rules are out the door when it comes to making luscious stuffing for pasta. To clean the machine after use, just wipe the parts with a soft brush.

Capelli D'Angelo and Quadrucci

- Capelli D'Angelo (angelhair): To make angelhair, follow the procedure above but cut the pasta as thinly as possible.

- Quadrucci: Cut the pasta for tagliatelle. As you unravel the ribbons, however, cut them crosswise into small squares.

- If you'll be storing the pasta (dry pasta keeps for months), wrap the ribbons or strips loosely around your hand into nests and put on a kitchen towel to dry. To use the same day, lay them flat.

Pappardelle and Farfalle

- Pappardelle: To make the saw-edged version of pappardelle, use a fluted pastry cutter on flat sheets of pasta.

- For straight-edged shapes, roll up the pasta (just like fettuccine) and cut ribbons ¼ inch wide.

- Farfalle: Cut a sheet of pasta into 1½-inch squares using a fluted pastry cutter. Pinch each square in the middle to make what looks like a butterfly, or perhaps a bowtie.

BRUSCHETTA

A favorite as an appetizer, bruschetta is both delicious and filling

The region of Umbria, Italy, is well known for bruschetta, or toasted bread. The difference between bruschetta and crostini is simply the thickness of the bread and the presentation. Crostini are thinner than bruschetta and look more elegant, while bruschetta, being thicker, are more commonly thought of as comfort food.

Bruschetta should be crispy on the outside and softer on the inside. If it's also crispy on the inside, it will break when you eat it instead of holding its shape. It's rubbed with fresh garlic and served with a generous drizzle of extra-virgin olive oil over the top. The perfect bread for bruschetta is crusty rustic type that can hold the fruity oil and the variety of toppings. It is great by itself or as an accompaniment for soups.
Yield: serves 6

Ingredients:

6 slices crusty Italian bread, about 1 inch thick

2-3 garlic cloves, peeled

Extra-virgin olive oil

Freshly ground black pepper

Bruschetta

- Grill the bread slices on an outdoor grill, or toast in an oven on a baking sheet, until nicely browned on both sides, about 5 minutes.

- Rub each slice, on one side only, with a whole clove of garlic.

- Place each bread slice on an individual serving plate, and drizzle with extra-virgin olive oil.

- Sprinkle freshly ground black pepper over the bread slices.

Tomato Bruschetta: Coarsely chop 2 ripe tomatoes and place them in a bowl with 1 clove finely minced garlic, 2 tablespoons olive oil, 1 tablespoon balsamic vinegar, 2 tablespoons minced fresh basil, and salt and pepper to taste. Stir gently to mix. Cut another ripe tomato in half; rub the cut side over the bread slices, then top with remaining tomato mixture. Serve immediately.

Cheese Bruschetta: Make the recipe as directed, except after rubbing the grilled bread with garlic, top it with a mixture of 1 cup shredded mozzarella cheese, ⅓ cup freshly grated Parmesan cheese, and 1 tablespoon minced fresh thyme leaves. Return the bread to the grill or oven and grill or toast until the cheese melts. Place on plates, add black pepper, and serve.

Grilling or Toasting Bread

- Whether you grill the bread over an open fire or toast it in the oven, watch it carefully to make sure it doesn't overbrown or burn.

- The thickness of the bread is very important. One-inch-thick slices are ideal for bruschetta.

- While the grilled or toasted bread is still warm, rub a garlic clove over one side of each slice.

Extra-Virgin Olive Oil

- There are several types of olive oil, ranging from pure to extra-virgin. Pure olive oil is great for frying food, while extra-virgin is preferred for finishing dishes that need a final drizzle of oil.

- With its rich green color and fresh flavor, extra-virgin olive oil is the best-quality olive oil.

- Drizzling the bruschetta with extra-virgin olive oil adds moisture and a desirable flavor.

ANTIPASTO

37

RED MINI BAKED POTATOES

Potatoes, loaded with protein, minerals, and vitamins, are an established part of Italian cuisine

The potato is a very versatile vegetable. It can be boiled, baked, grilled, or stuffed. Leftovers can be sliced and added to salads or served by themselves, with a little extra-virgin olive oil, a little vinegar, and salt and black pepper to taste. Potatoes are also used to make gnocchi.

Potatoes have long been popular in the Trentino and Alto Adige regions of Italy. People there claim that they are the first in Italy to adopt this vegetable and even the first to incorporate it in bread dough.

These miniature baked potatoes can be eaten with your hands. They are great as appetizers for a dinner party or as a snack.
Yield: serves 20

Ingredients:

20 small red potatoes

$1/4$ cup vegetable oil

Salt, to taste

$1/2$ cup sour cream

1 ounce Danish blue cheese, crumbled (if a milder blue cheese is preferred, try Gorgonzola)

2 tablespoons snipped fresh chives, for garnish

Red Mini Baked Potatoes

- Preheat the oven to 350°F. Prep the potatoes with the oil and salt (see technique).

- In a small bowl, combine the sour cream and blue cheese, mixing well.

- Add some of the blue cheese mixture to each potato.

- Place on a serving dish and garnish with the chives. Serve hot or at room temperature.

Potato Slices with Blue Cheese: Substitute 4 large russet potatoes for the small red potatoes. Cut the potatoes into ½-inch slices and toss with oil and salt. Spread in a single layer on a baking sheet and bake, turning once, at 400°F for 15 to 20 minutes until browned and tender. Remove from the oven; top with the blue cheese mixture and serve.

Potato Wedges with Blue Cheese Dip: Substitute Yukon Gold potatoes for the red potatoes. Cut each potato into six wedges and toss with oil and salt. Place on a cookie sheet and bake at 400°F for 30 minutes, until tender and golden brown around the edges. Double the amounts of sour cream and blue cheese and add ¼ cup light cream to thin. Serve with the blue cheese mixture.

Prepping the Potatoes

Adding Blue Cheese Mixture

- Wash and dry the potatoes. Toss them with oil in a bowl to coat well.

- Dip the potatoes in the salt for a light coating.

- Spread the potatoes out on a baking sheet.

- Bake the potatoes for 45 to 50 minutes, or until tender.

- Cut a cross in the top of each baked potato.

- Gently squeeze each potato with your fingers to open them up.

- Top each opened potato with a dollop of the blue cheese mixture.

ANTIPASTO

39

SEAFOOD SALAD

Fish is a constant in the Italian diet, and *insalata di mare* is a favorite

From ancient times, the nets of Mediterranean fishermen have been laden with a rich variety of seafood. Marinated cold fish dishes are an integral part of antipasti. The best way to buy fish is from a retailer that you trust. The fish should smell pleasantly of the sea but not be too pungent.

To determine freshness, use the thumb test: Press your thumb on the fish. It should spring immediately back into shape. If the indentation of the thumb remains, it means the fish is old.

This classic dish gives the hungry fish lover an opportunity to try different kinds. This salad is perfect as a meal by itself for those hot summer days.

Yield: serves 2

Ingredients:

Juice of 2 lemons

2 garlic cloves

2 pounds seafood, washed and cleaned (mussels, baby octopus, small squid, and clams)

$1/4$ cup olive oil

2 tablespoons finely chopped flat-leaf (Italian) parsley

Salt and pepper, to taste

Seafood Salad

- Pour the lemon juice over the garlic in a bowl; set aside for 1 hour. Then remove and discard the garlic.

- Cook the seafood in 1 cup of water, or enough water to cover the bottom of the pan, until the mussels and clams have opened.

- In a large serving bowl, combine the lemon juice–garlic mixture with the olive oil, parsley, salt, and pepper. Coat the seafood with this mixture and store in the refrigerator. Stir well before serving.

Preparing Seafood

Peeling Garlic

- Keep fresh seafood in the refrigerator until it's time to begin cooking.

- The mussels and clams need to be cleaned. Discard any shellfish that are open when raw. Check to see that the wiry beard has been removed from each mussel.

Rinse the shellfish in cold running water to remove any sand.

- When the mussels and clams open their shells, they are cooked. Discard any mussels or clams that do not open.

- To peel garlic, place a clove under the flat side of a chef's knife and carefully pound the flat surface with your fist.

- The paper-like skin will break apart, and you can then easily pull out the cloves.

- To get the garlic smell off your hands, rub them against a metal surface, such as a faucet, for 30 seconds.

ANTIPASTO

PROSCIUTTO WITH MELON

According to regulations, luscious San Daniele prosciutto can only be produced in Friuli, Italy

Friuli is one of the few regions of Italy that can boast a DOC ham (one whose place of origin is legally defined and controlled): prosciutto di San Daniele. According to regulations, controlled-origin hams can only be produced from freshly cut, locally produced meats.

Production methods have changed little with the passage of time. The selected cuts of meat are first trimmed, and the fat and rind removed. The curing time depends on the weight. After curing, the ham is pressed to reduce its moisture content and become more compact. This process accounts for the typical shape of the hams. *Yield: serves 4*

Ingredients:

1 large sweet melon

16 slices Parmigiano Reggiano cheese, cut very thin

16 slices San Daniele prosciutto, sliced very thin

Extra-virgin olive oil, to taste

Salt, to taste

Prosciutto with Melon

- Wash the melon well; cut the flesh away from the rind and cut each wedge in half to make 16 total pieces.

- Place the slices of cheese on top of the melon pieces.

- Wrap the prosciutto around the melon and cheese.

- Arrange on a large serving platter, drizzle with extra-virgin olive oil, sprinkle with salt, and serve.

Prosciutto with Figs: Make the recipe as directed, except use 8 fresh figs instead of the melon. Wash the figs well and slice them lengthwise, discarding the stems. Top with cheese and wrap prosciutto around the figs as described. Serve immediately.

Prosciutto with Papaya: Make the recipe as directed, except use 2 ripe papayas in place of the melon. Wash the skin and cut each papaya into 4 quarters. You can leave the seeds, or remove them, as they are slightly bitter. Top with 1 tablespoon mascarpone cheese and wrap the prosciutto around the papaya. Drizzle with olive oil and top with pepper; serve immediately.

Proper Pairings

- The pairing of melon and prosciutto is a classic Italian recipe. The salty ham also goes well with figs.

- A modern twist to this traditional dish calls for other tropical fruits such as papaya or mango.

- Simply peel the papaya and mango, then cut into slices. Wrap a slice of prosciutto around each piece of fruit.

Prosciutto Packages

- Because the prosciutto is sliced paper-thin, it's very easy to wrap it around the fruit and cheese. The prosciutto will cling to itself, resulting in an appetizer that holds together nicely.

- If desired, you can also drape a slice of prosciutto around larger pieces of fruit, such as a wedge of cantaloupe, for an impressive first course.

ANTIPASTO

MUSHROOM RAGU

The popular porcini mushroom is just one of the many varieties found under the trees

When I was very young, I remember going mushroom hunting with my siblings under the watchful eyes of my precious grandmother. She was the expert, and she knew how dangerous this could be. But under her supervision and after many years of practice, I have learned how to distinguish the edible mushrooms from the poisonous.

Button mushrooms are the common white mushrooms that are easy to find. Exotic mushrooms are also available in many supermarkets. Shiitake, portobello, chanterelle, and cremini are all worth trying. Mushrooms are an important part of the Italians' everyday diet.

Yield: serves 2

Ingredients:

2 pounds mixed fresh mushrooms

1 small bunch parsley

2 garlic cloves

5 tablespoons olive oil

3 tablespoons white wine

1/4 cup heavy cream

Mushroom Ragu

- Clean the mushrooms; trim and discard the woody stems. Wash and chop the parsley. Peel and quarter the garlic cloves.

- Heat the olive oil in a heavy pan. Add the garlic and sauté for 2 minutes. Add the mushrooms and fry briefly.

- Reduce the heat and pour in the white wine; cook for 2 minutes, then add the cream.

- Braise the mushrooms until they are soft. Sprinkle with parsley.

Cleaning Mushrooms

- To wash or not to wash the mushrooms is an age-old question.

- Many chefs believe mushrooms should never be washed because they will soak up water like a sponge.

- Food scientists say this is not true and that mush-

rooms can be rinsed in cold water just before cooking.

- But everyone agrees you should not rinse mushrooms if they are being used raw. Instead, use a mushroom brush or a paper towel to gently remove any visible dirt particles.

Braising Mushrooms

- After briefly frying the mushrooms, add the liquids to the pan.

- Cover and reduce the heat to medium-low. The mushrooms should be simmering in the sauce.

- Cook the mushrooms until they are tender, approximately 8 to 10 minutes, stirring twice.

ANTIPASTO

TUSCAN ARTICHOKE LEAVES
Ancients Romans thought the artichoke was a creation of the gods

Ancient Romans were convinced that artichokes had powers to purify the blood. They were so expensive that only the rich could afford them.

Today artichokes are within everybody's means. You don't even need utensils to eat the vegetable—just pull the leaves off with your fingers, dip the tender ends in sauce, and scrape off the flesh with your teeth. What's left of the leaves can then be deposited on a plate provided for this purpose. After all leaves are pulled, the hairy choke is visible and can be discarded, leaving exposed the really yummy part, the heart. Sprinkle this with vinaigrette and eat with a knife and fork.
Yield: serves 20

KNACK ITALIAN COOKING

Ingredients:

3 large green artichokes

1 cup freshly grated Parmesan cheese

1 cup fresh bread crumbs

Olive oil for sautéing

4 eggs, lightly beaten

Tuscan Artichoke Leaves

- Trim the artichokes. Boil or steam them until the leaves are tender, 30 to 40 minutes. Remove the artichokes from the pot and cool.

- Mix the Parmesan cheese and bread crumbs in a bowl.

- Remove the leaves from the artichokes, discarding all the small leaves from the center and scooping out the hairy center. Cut the hearts into six pieces.

- Heat ¾ inch olive oil in a heavy skillet. Dip the artichokes in the egg and then parmesan bread crumb mixture and sauté the pieces; drain and serve.

• • • • RECIPE VARIATION • • • •

Gorgonzola Dip: A few hours before preparing the artichokes, beat ¼ cup (½ stick) butter with ¼ cup ricotta cheese in small bowl. Add 1 cup crumbly Gorgonzola or other good-quality sharp blue cheese along with 2 teaspoons minced fresh oregano. Cover and refrigerate. Prepare the artichoke leaves as directed, and serve them hot with this cheese dip.

Trimming Artichokes

Dipping Artichoke Hearts

- Before cooking, you will need to trim the artichokes.

- With kitchen shears, trim the prickly point from the tip of each artichoke leaf, skipping the top two rows.

- Place the artichoke on a cutting board, holding the stem with one hand. With your other hand, cut off the top two rows with a sharp chef's knife.

- The stem can now be cut flush with the base of the bulb. Place the trimmed artichokes in a bowl of acidulated water.

- Dip each artichoke heart piece into the beaten eggs, and then into the bread crumb and cheese mixture.

- Sauté the pieces in the hot oil in a single layer, turning once, until they become golden in color.

- Drain on paper towels.

ANTIPASTO

WEDDING SOUP WITH MEATBALLS

A traditional Italian favorite, this soup nourishes both body and soul

Italian soups can be meals in themselves. They can be hearty or delicate, depending on the amount of liquid added. This specific soup is hearty and one of my favorites because it reminds me of my childhood with my beloved grandmother. I would help her make this soup from scratch. I loved tagging along with her throughout the day, collecting the various ingredients.

Homemade soups provide a healthier alternative to the store-bought, canned variety that's loaded with sodium. This is my version of my grandmother's soup, with its full flavor intact, updated for today's busier times.

Yield: serves 6–8

KNACK ITALIAN COOKING

Ingredients:

Meatballs:

$1/2$ pound ground veal

$1/2$ pound ground sirloin

$1/4$ cup bread crumbs

1 large egg, lightly beaten

1 teaspoon grated lemon zest

1 teaspoon grated nutmeg

1 tablespoon chopped fresh parsley

Salt and freshly ground pepper, to taste

Soup:

4 cups chicken or beef broth

2 cups spinach, washed and cut into pieces

$1/4$ cup (or more if you like) grated Pecorino Romano cheese

Wedding Soup with Meatballs

- Preheat the oven to 350°F. Form the meatballs (see technique). Bake for 30 minutes. Drain off the extra fat.

- In a large pot, bring the broth to a boil. Add the spinach, cover, and simmer for 5 minutes.

- Add the meatballs to the hot broth and return to a simmer.

- Stir in the cheese, and serve immediately.

Lighter Wedding Soup: Prepare the recipe as directed, replacing the veal and sirloin with 1 pound ground mixed dark- and white-meat turkey. Add 2 minced garlic cloves to the meat mixture; bake for 15 to 20 minutes, until done. Use chicken broth for the liquid and add 2 tablespoons minced fresh basil leaves along with the Pecorino Romano cheese. Serve with toasted Italian bread.

Rich Wedding Soup: Prepare the recipe as directed, except use ½ pound sirloin, ¼ pound minced prosciutto, and ⅓ pound mild Italian sausages in place of the veal and sirloin. Use beef broth as the liquid. Add 2 sprigs fresh thyme, 1 sprig fresh rosemary, and ⅓ cup chopped celery leaves to the broth along with the spinach. Remove the thyme and rosemary stems before serving the soup.

Forming Meatballs

Preparing Broth

- In a large bowl, combine the ground meat, bread crumbs, egg, lemon zest, nutmeg, parsley, salt, and pepper. Mix well using a fork or your hands.

- With your hands, form small marble-size balls (approximately three dozen), and place them on a rimmed baking sheet.

- When the broth comes to a boil, toss in the spinach. Make sure the spinach is torn into pieces and that all the stems have been removed.

- The spinach will wilt almost immediately. Reduce the heat, and allow the broth to simmer so that the taste and flavor will intensify.

SOUPS

SPEEDY MINESTRONE

This hearty, healthy soup makes a perfect quick dinner—especially if you chop the vegetables ahead of time

Most people have heard of the classic minestrone, or "big soup," so called because of the variety and amounts of vegetables that go into it. Usually this soup is eaten hot, but in some regions of Italy, such as Campania, the soup is eaten at room temperature during the summer.

Each region adds its own flair to the soup. In the Veneto region of Italy, rice is added. Tuscans make a hearty minestrone thickened with beans and bread. Romans drop a mixture of egg and Parmesan cheese into the hot soup, while southern Italians love stylish ditalini in their soup.

You'll find a vast variety of vegetables in supermarkets for this soup. *Yield: serves 4–6*

Ingredients:

1 1/2 quarts (6 cups) vegetable stock

1 pound all-purpose potatoes, cut into small cubes

1 baby leek, rinsed well and cut into strips

2 medium carrots, cut into bite-size slices

2 small zucchini, cut into bite-size slices

2 celery stalks, chopped

2 ripe tomatoes, peeled and cubed

1 small can (8 ounces) beans, drained and rinsed (white, kidney, or garbanzo)

Salt and freshly ground pepper

2 teaspoons basil or parsley pesto (store-bought is fine)

2 ounces Parmesan or Romano cheese, freshly grated

Speedy Minestrone

- Pour the stock into a large pot, cover, and bring to a boil.

- Toss in the cut-up potatoes, leeks, carrots, zucchini, and celery. Add the tomatoes to the pot along with the drained beans.

- Cover the pot, and continue simmering the soup for 15 to 20 minutes over low heat.

- Add salt and pepper to taste. Stir in the pesto and grated cheese. Serve with garlic bread, if desired.

Ribollita: Make the soup as directed, omitting the pesto and cheese. Add 1 tablespoon tomato paste. Cool the soup and refrigerate. The next day, stir in 2 cups cubed stale crusty Italian bread, such as ciabatta; reheat the soup until the bread dissolves and the soup thickens. Serve with Parmesan cheese and drizzle with extra-virgin olive oil. This is a good way to use up leftover soup.

Southern Minestrone: Prepare the recipe but double the amount of canned beans and triple the amount of pesto. Add 1 small chopped onion to the soup mixture along with rest of the vegetables. When the veggies are tender, add 1 cup ditalini or other small pasta; bring to a simmer and cook for 8 to 9 minutes, until the pasta is al dente. Stir in the pesto and cheese; season to taste.

Preparing the Vegetables

Peeling Tomatoes

- Wash the potatoes, peel them, and cut them into cubes.

- Slit the leek lengthwise down the center, rinse it well (make sure to get all the sand that's stuck between the layers), and cut it into strips.

- Peel the carrots, and cut them into slices. Wash the zucchini and celery stalks, and cut into strips or slices.

- Add all the prepared vegetables to the boiling broth.

- Plunge cored ripe tomatoes into a pot of boiling water for 15 seconds. With a slotted spoon, remove the tomatoes from the water. Put them immediately in bowl of ice-cold water to stop the cooking process.

- With a paring knife, remove the skin from each tomato. It should slip off easily.

- The skin will slide right off your knife when you dip it into the cold water.

SOUPS

ROASTED BUTTERNUT SQUASH SOUP

With a green salad, this rich wintry soup is supper for the whole family

When squash, with its myriad colors, appears at the farmer's market, the holidays are not far behind. The squash family is a vast one and plays an important role in Italian cuisine. Squashes can be braised, sautéed, tossed in flour and fried, broiled, stuffed, or used as a salad or dessert ingredient. The possibilities are almost endless. The long green zucchini in particular have had much success not just in Italy but throughout the world.

Squash is hard to peel, but the hard shell helps to keep the vegetable ripe in cold places longer. Butternut squash flesh is dense and moist, much like yams; its flavor is the most intense of all the winter squashes. *Yield: serves 4*

Ingredients:

2 tablespoons extra-virgin olive oil

¹/₂ cup diced onion (¹/₄-inch cubes)

¹/₄ cup diced celery (¹/₄-inch cubes)

¹/₄ cup diced carrot (¹/₄-inch cubes)

1 cinnamon stick

Salt and ground pepper

4 cups low-salt chicken stock, canned or homemade

¹/₂ teaspoon ground coriander

1¹/₂ cups roasted winter squash

¹/₂ cup half-and-half (optional)

¹/₄ cup mascarpone cheese

2 tablespoons toasted pumpkin seeds

Roasted Butternut Squash Soup

- In a large saucepan, heat oil over a medium flame. Add the onion, celery, carrot, and cinnamon stick; sauté until soft, about 10 minutes.

- Add the stock and coriander; bring to a boil, then simmer. Stir in the squash, and simmer for 10 minutes. Discard the cinnamon stick.

- When the soup is cool, puree it in a blender. Return the soup to the pan and reheat gently. Add half-and-half, if desired. Season with salt and pepper.

- Ladle into four soup bowls. Garnish with spoonful of mascarpone and pumpkin seeds.

Creamy Acorn Squash Soup: Prepare the recipe, except use 1 peeled, cubed, and seeded acorn squash in place of the butternut squash. Omit the cinnamon, coriander, and mascarpone; add ¼ teaspoon freshly grated nutmeg. When blending the soup, add 3 ounces cream cheese and the half-and-half. Pour the mixture back into the pot and reheat gently. Garnish with pumpkin seeds.

Rich Butternut Squash Soup: Make the soup as directed, but double the mascarpone. Omit the coriander; add ⅛ teaspoon ground cloves. When the vegetables are tender, puree the soup with the mascarpone using an immersion blender. You can chill this soup until cold. Thin, if necessary, with more chicken stock before serving.

Roasting Winter Squash

Toasting Seeds

- Preheat the oven to 400°F.

- Peel the squash with a vegetable peeler.

- Cut it in half lengthwise, discard the seeds, cut into 1-inch dices, place in a bowl, and season with salt and pepper.

- Place the diced squash on a baking sheet in a single layer and bake for 1 hour; set aside until cool enough to handle.

- If you don't want to use a fresh pumpkin, you can always purchase seeds at the store. Place ½ cup pumpkin seeds and 1 tablespoon extra-virgin olive oil in a small skillet over medium heat.

- Cook, turning the seeds often, until they pop, puff, and turn brown and crispy; add salt and toss.

- Store in an airtight container in a cool dry place, or freeze the toasted seeds.

SOUPS

THREE-ONION SOUP

This soup's distinct onion flavor makes it the perfect dish for fall

The family of onions is more extensive than just the ones you'll use in this dish. It includes yellow, white, sweet, and red onions, along with shallots, scallions, leeks, and garlic. The harvest of onions begins in the spring and lasts through the fall. Buy a lot, caramelize them, and freeze for later use.

Yellow onions, leeks, and garlic are the three onion family members combined in this full-flavored soup. For a heartier rendition, toast slices of country-style bread on both sides until golden, and rub them on one side with whole garlic cloves. Place a slice of bread in the bottom of each soup bowl, and ladle the soup over the bread.

Yield: serves 6

Ingredients:

3 tablespoons extra-virgin olive oil

4 large yellow onions, diced

4 leeks, carefully rinsed and diced

3 ounces pancetta, finely diced

5 garlic cloves

6 cups low-salt chicken stock

1¹/₄ cups fruity red wine, such as Chianti or Zinfandel

2 tablespoons balsamic vinegar

1 tablespoon red wine vinegar

Salt and ground pepper

1 cup freshly grated Parmesan cheese

Three-Onion Soup

- In a soup pot over medium heat, warm the oil. Add the onions, leeks, and pancetta. Sauté, stirring occasionally, until the onions and leeks are soft, about 10 minutes.

- Add the garlic and sauté, stirring, for 1 minute. Add the stock and wine; simmer, uncovered, over medium-low heat until the vegetables are very soft, about 30 minutes.

- Just before serving, stir in the balsamic and red wine vinegars; season with salt and pepper. Ladle the soup into bowls. Sprinkle with Parmesan cheese.

· · · · RECIPE VARIATION · · · ·

Five-Onion Soup: Prepare the recipe as directed, except substitute 4 shallots for 1 of the yellow onions. Peel and dice the shallots and cook with the onion, leeks, and pancetta. Use beef broth or stock in place of the chicken stock. When the soup has cooled, top with the Parmesan cheese and ½ cup finely snipped fresh chives.

Sauté in a Soup Pot

- One of the secrets to fast and easy cooking is one-pot recipes such as this.

- Instead of using a sauté pan, start cooking the onions, leeks, and pancetta in a pot large enough to hold all the remaining ingredients.

- As you continue with the recipe, you can easily add the stock and wine, building layers of flavors in just one large soup pot.

Adding the Vinegar

- Whenever you add bold ingredients such as balsamic and red wine vinegar to a dish, it's best to do so toward the end of the cooking time.

- This ensures that those particular flavors will be fresh and detectable, not lost in a long cooking process.

SOUPS

ASPARAGUS SOUP WITH LOBSTER

Lobster and asparagus—this combination will make you feel festive any day of the week

May is the best month for catching lobsters off the Sardinian coast. This delectable meat does not need elaborate cooking; it already has a wonderful flavor on its own. Lobsters are delicious barbecued, or baked in the oven with olives, salt, pepper, and rosemary. They require only a short time to cook.

The appearance of asparagus in the market signals the beginning of spring. Stalks should be firm, straight, and not wilted. The cut base should be moist, and the leaves that form the tips should be tightly closed.

A warm bowl of this elegant soup is a welcome treat in the cold winter. The herbal flavor of asparagus is a good match for the sweetness of the lobster meat. *Yield: serves 4*

KNACK ITALIAN COOKING

Ingredients:

1 leek, rinsed well and chopped (including green tops)

3 shallots, peeled and chopped

2 tablespoons olive oil

³/₄ cup water, divided

¹/₄ teaspoon salt

¹/₄ teaspoon freshly ground pepper

1 cup low-sodium vegetable or chicken broth

1 pound asparagus, cut into 1-inch pieces, ends discarded (reserve 12 tips for garnish)

8 ounces lobster meat, cooked and shelled (fresh or frozen)

Garnish:

1 sprig lemon thyme, chopped

1 sprig parsley, chopped

Asparagus Soup with Lobster

- In a large saucepan, combine the leeks, shallots, olive oil, ¼ cup water, salt, and pepper.

- Cover and simmer over low heat until all the vegetables are soft, 30 minutes.

- In a separate pot, bring the broth to a boil; set aside.

- Add the asparagus to the leek mixture, and cook until al dente. Puree (see technique).

- To serve, mound the lobster in four soup bowls. Ladle soup around the lobster, and garnish each bowl with lemon thyme, parsley, and asparagus tips.

About Lobster: Lobster isn't difficult to prepare, but it does take some effort. Make sure the lobster you buy is alive, then plunge it into boiling water. When the lobster is done, it will turn bright red. Split it down the middle and remove the meat from the body, claws, and tail. You can also buy prepared lobster meat from the butcher; you may need to order it ahead of time.

· · · · RECIPE VARIATION · · · ·

Seafood Asparagus Soup: Prepare the recipe as directed, except substitute ¼ pound small cooked shrimp and ¼ pound lump crabmeat for the lobster. Peel and devein the shrimp, and pick over the crabmeat to remove any cartilage before adding to the soup. Omit the lemon thyme; add 2 tablespoons minced fresh basil leaves.

Asparagus

- If you hold an asparagus spear in the right way, the tough woody part of the stem will break off in just the right place.

- Hold the spear with one hand. With your other hand, hold the woody end of the spear. Bend the spear until it snaps.

- Or you can cut off the woody stems, and use a vegetable peeler to shave away any tough strands.

Pureeing Mixture

- To puree means to start with a solid food and reduce it to a smooth consistency.

- Ingredients need to be at least partially cooked before pureeing. You can puree in a food processor or a blender.

- Add the asparagus–leek mixture to a blender with the reserved broth and remaining ½ cup water. Puree until smooth.

- Strain through a fine sieve, forcing out as much liquid as possible.

SOUPS

BROCCOLI & GORGONZOLA SOUP

The creamy tang of Gorgonzola combined with broccoli makes this a soup worth waiting for

When scientists learned that broccoli may protect against cancer, the vegetable saw a sharp a rise in popularity. Broccoli adapts particularly well to cheese. Because it's so flavorful by itself, few additional ingredients are required to turn it into a tasty soup. However, the creamy tang of the Gorgonzola cheese makes this one quite special.

Gorgonzola ripens in three to six months and has a fat content of 48 percent. It's usually wrapped in foil to keep it moist. Gorgonzola comes from the Lombardy region of Italy. It has a red to orange rind covered with powdery patches of gray and blue mold. It's often used as a table cheese, in dressings and salads, or on pasta or gnocchi. *Yield: serves 4*

Ingredients:

2 tablespoons butter

1 onion, chopped

1 potato, peeled and chopped

2 heads broccoli, chopped

4 cups water

6 ounces Gorgonzola cheese, cubed

Freshly grated nutmeg, to taste

Salt and ground black pepper

Walnut oil, as needed

Broccoli and Gorgonzola Soup

- Heat the butter in a large saucepan; stir in the onion and potatoes. Cover and cook over low heat for 5 minutes. Add the broccoli and cook for another 5 minutes. Add the water, bring to a boil, season, and simmer for 15 minutes.

- Strain, reserving the liquid.

- Puree (see technique). Pour the soup and reserved liquid into a clean saucepan. Reheat until nearly boiling, then remove from the heat.

- Stir in the cheese until melted. Add nutmeg, salt, and pepper to taste. Serve in four warmed bowls drizzled with walnut oil.

Onion Bruschetta: Peel and chop 2 yellow onions. Cook in 2 tablespoons butter and 1 tablespoon olive oil until tender. Reduce the heat to low and simmer for 15 to 20 minutes until the onion is golden brown. Slice and toast Italian bread and drizzle with olive oil. Top with the onion mixture and ½ cup grated Parmesan cheese. Toast under a broiler until the cheese melts; serve with soup.

Spinach & Gorgonzola Soup: Prepare recipe except substitute 2 pounds of fresh baby spinach leaves for broccoli, and use chicken stock instead of water. After cooking onion and potato, add stock; bring to a boil, reduce heat, and simmer for 10 minutes until potato is tender. Add spinach and cook until wilted. Puree with an immersion blender, strain into a saucepan, then continue recipe.

Preparing the Broccoli

- Rinse the large heads of broccoli. Cut off the hard ends of each stalk. Remove any long leaves.

- Cut the stalks into 1-inch slices. Break apart the florets.

- Because this will all be cooked and pureed, you do not have to fuss with the individual florets. A rough chop will be fine.

Processing Vegetables

- Put the cooked vegetables in a food processor, and moisten with some of the cooking liquid.

- Process until the mixture is very silky and smooth. With the motor running, gradually add the remaining cooking liquid through the feed tube. Pour the soup into a clean saucepan.

SOUPS

ARUGULA SALAD

The fresh ingredients found in this delectable salad allow for easy digestion

Campo di Fiori, a fresh food market found in Rome that abounds with vendors who speak in the traditional Roman dialect, provides some of the best ingredients for Italian dishes. You can find fresh ingredients, however, without having to make the pilgrimage to Italy.

Italian foods consist mostly of fresh ingredients, especially fresh vegetables and fruit. Formerly a well-kept Italian secret, arugula is now known worldwide and can be found in your neighborhood supermarket.

Arugula is impressive, elegant, and quick to fix for dinner. One bunch is just right, even for a small appetite.

Yield: serves 4 as a starter

Ingredients:

3–4 bunches arugula (approximately 10 ounces)

2 tablespoons balsamic vinegar

Salt and freshly ground pepper

¼ cup olive oil

10 oil-packed sun-dried tomatoes, with 1–2 tablespoons of their oil

2 thin slices sandwich bread, cubed

1 garlic clove, minced

1–2 tablespoons capers, drained

Arugula Salad

- Cut off any coarse arugula stems, rinse the leaves, and drain in a colander.

- In a small bowl, whisk together the balsamic vinegar, salt, pepper, and olive oil. Set aside.

- Cut the tomatoes into strips. Heat the tomato oil in a skillet, and sauté the bread cubes in it over medium heat until brown. Add the garlic and stir.

- Place the arugula in a salad bowl, and pour the dressing over it. Toss well; scatter the tomato strips, capers, and bread cubes on top.

•••••••••• GREEN ● LIGHT ••••••••••

Try complementing this meal with a light, dry white wine and crusty French bread or olive bread. The bread can be toasted and rubbed with garlic before serving, or served as is with some olive oil for dipping. At only 150 calories per serving, this meal is perfect for a light lunch or dinner. Buon appetito!

•••• RECIPE VARIATION ••••

Cheese and Nut Arugula Salad: Prepare recipe except instead of tomatoes and croutons, scatter 2 tablespoons pine nuts (toasted quickly in a hot dry skillet for 1 to 2 minutes) and 2–4 tablespoons coarsely grated Parmesan on top of the arugula. Add the dressing, toss, and serve immediately.

Sun-Dried Tomatoes

- Sun-dried tomatoes are more popular in the United States than in Italy. Many commercially produced varieties are available in supermarkets and gourmet stores.

- The oil in which the sun-dried tomatoes are packed can be used to flavor vinaigrettes or to brush on bruschetta.

- Many cooks prefer to make their own oven-roasted tomatoes, which are intensely flavorful.

Making Croutons

- It's easy to make your own Italian croutons.

- In a skillet over medium heat, warm 1–2 tablespoons of the oil in which sun-dried tomatoes are packed. Slice fresh bread into bite-size cubes. Sauté the bread cubes in the tomato oil, turning often, until brown.

- Add the minced garlic to the skillet and stir. Be careful not to burn the garlic.

CAESAR SALAD

I bet you thought Caesar salad was named for the emperor of Rome

The story goes that Cesar Cardini was born in Italy in 1896 and emigrated with his brother Alex to the United States after World War I. They lived in San Diego but, to get around Prohibition laws, opened a restaurant in Tijuana, Mexico.

One particular busy day, they were short on supplies and did not want to disappoint their customers by sending them home with empty stomachs. On the spur of the moment,

Cesar collected a few of the ingredients he did have on hand, and for a dramatic effect he prepared this salad at the customers' tables.

Many others have also claimed the first Caesar salad, including Cesar's own brother. The salad's origins have never been proved definitively.

Yield: serves 4 as a starter

Ingredients:

1 large head romaine lettuce, rinsed and torn into pieces

4 ounces smoked bacon, cut into strips

3 tablespoons vegetable oil

2 thin slices white sandwich bread, cubed

2 garlic cloves, minced

2 eggs (as fresh as possible), boiled in their shells for 1 minute (see technique)

2–4 tablespoons fresh lemon juice

$^1/_3$ cup olive oil

2–3 teaspoons Worcestershire sauce

Salt and freshly ground pepper

2 anchovy fillets

2-ounce chunk Parmesan cheese

Caesar Salad

- Place the lettuce in a large salad bowl. Sauté the bacon in a skillet over medium heat until crisp; remove from the skillet. Add the vegetable oil and sauté the bread cubes until crispy. Add the garlic and stir.

- In a bowl, whisk the eggs with the lemon juice, olive oil, and Worcestershire sauce; season with salt and pepper. Pour the dressing over the lettuce.

- Chop the anchovy fillets; scatter atop the salad with the bacon and croutons. Coarsely grate Parmesan over the top.

• • • • RECIPE VARIATION • • • •

Chicken Caesar Salad: Prepare recipe but add 2 boneless, skinless chicken breasts. When bacon is removed from skillet, add oil and chicken and cook for 10 to 12 minutes, turning once, until chicken is thoroughly cooked. Remove chicken from skillet and continue with recipe. Let chicken stand for 5 minutes, then cut it into slices or cubes. Top the finished salad with the chicken.

• • • • • • • RED ● LIGHT • • • • • • •

Egg Safety: Since you're using raw eggs in this recipe, be sure they're very fresh and from an impeccable source. If you aren't sure about the quality, use pasteurized eggs—eggs that have been heated to 140°F. This doesn't cook eggs, but it does allow them to be safely used raw. Eggs have very specific expiration dates; follow them to the letter.

Preparing Ingredients

- Drain anchovy fillets, pat dry, and set aside in a bowl.

- Remove the coarse ribs from the lettuce; wash the leaves, drain in a colander, and dry well.

- Cut the lettuce leaves diagonally into ¾-inch strips.

- Place the cut-up lettuce in a large salad bowl, and toss with the dressing.

Preparing the Eggs

- With a pushpin, carefully prick a hole in the eggs and place them in boiling water for 1 minute, maximum.

- Then dunk the eggs in ice-cold water. Allow to cool.

- Crack the eggs open, and pour the still-liquid contents into a medium-size bowl.

MOZZARELLA & DRIED TOMATO SALAD

This fresh cheese should be eaten within a few days of being made

At first glance this recipe may seem intimidating because of the dried tomatoes, but it's actually quite simple—you just need to start a few days ahead in order to give the tomatoes plenty of time to dry out.

Tomatoes can be dried in the oven or in a dehydrator. Wash and dry the tomatoes, cut them in half lengthwise, and place them cut-side down on a rack placed on a baking sheet. Place

the rack in a 225°F oven, and bake the tomatoes until they resemble dried apricots. This could take up to 2 days.

When the tomatoes are ready, let them cool. Then layer the thawed dried tomatoes in jars, fill with olive oil, and add a few leaves of basil. Close the jars and let them rest in the refrigerator for up to half a day. Check the jars every 3 hours, adding more oil if necessary. *Yield: serves 4*

Ingredients:

$1/2$ pound fresh mozzarella cheese, thinly sliced

$1/3$ cup oil-packed dried tomatoes, coarsely chopped (reserve the oil)

$1/4$ cup fresh basil leaves torn in pieces

Salt and freshly ground pepper, to taste

2 tablespoons red wine vinegar

Insalata di Mozzarella

- Arrange the mozzarella in a shallow serving dish, overlapping the slices in an attractive pattern.

- Over the mozzarella, sprinkle the chopped dried tomatoes and about ½ cup of the tomato oil.

- Sprinkle the mozzarella with the fresh basil, salt, pepper, and red wine vinegar.

ZOOM

Fresh mozzarella cheese is as different from the part-skim processed cheese you buy in the supermarket as day is from night. Fresh mozzarella is milky and sweet, with a very mild taste. It's usually found packed in water, whey, or a mild brine. Look for it in Italian delis. Smoked mozzarella can be substituted for the fresh cheese.

Fresh Mozzarella

- Mozzarella is a soft fresh cheese made from cow's or buffalo's milk. The prized mozzarella made from buffalo's milk is called mozzarella di bufala.

- Mozzarella comes in a variety of shapes—rounds, braids, basket shapes, and balls, both large and small. The small balls of mozzarella are called bocconcini.

Before You Eat . . .

- This dish needs to be prepared well before mealtime. Before serving, cover the salad with plastic wrap and let it sit at least 3 hours at room temperature.

- While the salad is sitting, be sure to tilt and turn the dish now and then so that the juices flow over and around the cheese.

TRICOLOR SALAD

This salad is an homage to the Italian flag: green (avocado), white (mozzarella), and red (tomatoes)

This popular salad depends on the quality of its ingredients for its success. Mozzarella di bufala is best, if it's available.

Fresh cheeses are added to recipes for both texture and flavor. Mozzarella will absorb the tastes of other ingredients, giving the dish the intensity we all love.

Whole ripe plum tomatoes (on-the-vine tomatoes are the best) give up their juices to blend with extra-virgin olive oil for a natural dressing. Avocadoes can be grilled. Place the avocadoes on the grill cut-side down for 2 minutes or until the edges turn a little brown; turn them over and grill for 2 minutes more. The goal is to warm the fruit, not cook it.
Yield: serves 2

Ingredients:

5 ounces mozzarella di bufala

4 large plum tomatoes, sliced

Salt, to taste

1 large avocado

12 basil leaves

¼ cup extra-virgin olive oil

Ground black pepper

Tricolor Salad

- Arrange the sliced cheese and tomatoes on two salad plates.

- Sprinkle with salt (to taste). Set aside in a cool place to marinate for about 30 minutes.

- Pit, peel, and slice the avocado. Place it on top of the salad, and sprinkle with the basil.

- Drizzle with olive oil; add a little more salt and black pepper, if desired. Serve at room temperature, with crusty Italian bread.

• • • • RECIPE VARIATIONS • • • •

Tangy Onion Tricolor Salad: Prepare the recipe as directed, except add 1 large sweet red or purple onion. Peel the onion and slice into very thin rings. Separate the rings and scatter over the composed salad. In a small bowl, combine the olive oil with 2 tablespoons balsamic vinegar, salt, and pepper; whisk until combined. Drizzle over the salad and serve immediately.

Pisello Tricolor Salad: Prepare the recipe as directed, replacing the avocado with 1 cup frozen baby sweet peas. Place the peas in a colander and run hot water over them for 2 to 3 minutes until thawed. Drain on paper towels. Arrange the mozzarella and tomatoes on plates; sprinkle with salt and let stand. Top with the peas, basil, olive oil, and 1 tablespoon lemon juice.

Pitting the Avocado

- Just before serving, cut the avocado in half using a large sharp knife. Twist the avocado to separate.

- To remove the pit easily, strike it hard with the knife, which will become lodged in the pit. You can then use the knife to lift out the pit and discard it. Peel the avocado, and it's ready for slicing.

Scooping and Slicing the Avocado

- Once an avocado has been pitted and peeled, place each half cut-side down on a cutting board.

- With a sharp knife, slice the avocado lengthwise for long strips or horizontally for half-moons. You can also cut the avocado into chunks or cubes.

PEAR & PARMESAN SALAD

Sweet pears and sharp Parmigiano Reggiano make a great pair

There are a variety of pears out there. Bartletts are medium-size, bell-shaped fruits with a pale green to golden and sometimes red skin. Sweet and juicy, with a creamy texture, Bartletts are good for eating, cooking, and preserving; they're available from early summer to early November.

Anjous are large, plump pears with short necks and red-yellow skin. They have a medium to coarse texture, and are juicy with a hint of spice. They're best for cooking when slightly underripe, and can be eaten raw when ripe. They are available from autumn to early winter.

Comice pears are large, round, and red-tinged, with greenish yellow skin and soft, juicy aromatic flesh. They are usually eaten raw and are available from midsummer through late autumn. *Yield: serves 4*

Ingredients:

4 ripe pears

Dressing:

2 tablespoons extra-virgin olive oil

1 tablespoon sunflower oil

2 tablespoons cider vinegar or white wine vinegar

1/2 teaspoon light brown sugar

Generous pinch dried thyme

Salt and black pepper

1 tablespoon poppy seeds

Watercress to garnish

2-ounce chunk Parmesan cheese

Water crackers or rye bread, as needed

Pear and Parmesan Salad

- Prep the pears (see technique).

- To make the dressing, combine the oils, vinegar, sugar, thyme, and seasoning in a bowl. Mix well. Add the poppy seeds. Drizzle the dressing over the pears.

- Garnish with watercress, shaving Parmesan over the top. Serve with water crackers or thinly sliced rye bread.

• • • • RECIPE VARIATIONS • • • •

Pear & Gorgonzola Salad: Prepare the recipe as directed, except substitute about 4 ounces of Gorgonzola, Gorgonzola dolce (sweet), Danish blue, or Stilton for the Parmesan cheese. Crumble the cheese over the top of the salad and serve immediately, perhaps adding some toasted pine nuts or toasted hazelnuts for crunch.

To toast nuts, spread them on a cookie sheet in a single layer. Bake at 350°F for 12 to 18 minutes, shaking the pan occasionally, until the nuts are fragrant and start to brown. Do not let them burn. Or you can toast the nuts in a dry skillet over medium heat for 3 to 6 minutes. Let the nuts cool completely before chopping or they can become oily and soggy.

Prepping Pears

- Rinse the pears under cold running water, and dry with paper towels. Peel the pears, if desired.

- Cut each pear lengthwise into quarters, and remove the cores.

- Cut each pear quarter in half lengthwise. Arrange them in a pleasing pattern on four small serving plates.

Mixing the Dressing

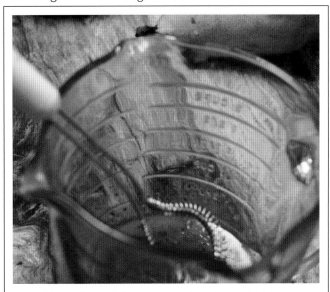

- Freshly made salad dressings are easy to prepare, and the ingredients are readily available.

- Combine the oil and vinegar in a medium-size bowl. Use a whisk to emulsify the mixture. Add the main flavor ingredients, mixing well. Always add fresh herbs last.

- Store any leftover dressing in the refrigerator.

ROASTED VEGETABLES W/PECORINO

A colorful medley of the finest fresh veggies

Italy's food is based on one critical factor: freshness. Vegetables are always in season somewhere in Italy. Everywhere you go, you can see on people's faces the enthusiasm they have for planting their gardens, the way they use every inch of their yard for this purpose, the care they devote to their plants' needs throughout the growing season.

Vegetables are cooked in as many ways as your imagination allows: baked, fried, grilled, stuffed, raw for salads, and so on. Wise cooks use what's in season and keep preparations simple to let the flavors shine through.

Eggplant, zucchini, bell peppers, and tomatoes make the best medley when roasted and then drizzled with fragrant olive oil. Shavings of Pecorino add a perfect finishing touch. *Yield: serves 4–6*

Ingredients:

1 eggplant, sliced

2 zucchini, sliced

2 bell peppers (one red, one yellow), cored and quartered

1 large onion, thickly sliced

2 large carrots, cut into sticks

4 firm plum tomatoes, cut in half

Extra-virgin olive oil, as needed

Salt and ground black pepper

3 tablespoons chopped fresh parsley

3 tablespoons pine nuts, toasted

5-ounce chunk Pecorino Romano cheese

Crusty bread (optional)

Roasted Vegetables with Pecorino

- Preheat the oven to 425°F.

- Prepare the eggplant. Spread cut-up vegetables in a large roasting pan. Brush lightly with oil and roast for about 20 minutes.

- Transfer the vegetables to large serving platter. Peel the blackened peppers.

- Drizzle vegetables with juices from roasting pan; season with salt and pepper. As they cool, sprinkle with more oil. At room temperature, sprinkle with parsley and pine nuts.

- Shave cheese over the vegetables. Serve with crusty bread, if desired.

• • • • RECIPE VARIATIONS • • • •

Roasted Vegetables with Manchego: You can substitute any hard sheep's-milk cheese for the Pecorino. Many types blend well with the rich flavors of the vegetables and herbs. Try Spanish Manchego or British Malvern, thinly sliced with a vegetable peeler. Or use Parmigiano Reggiano cheese or a hard grated Asiago cheese.

Roasted Vegetable Salad: Prepare the recipe as directed, but when the vegetables are cool, place them in a bowl with 1 cup torn fresh basil leaves, 2 cups arugula leaves, and 2 cups cooked tortellini pasta. In small bowl, combine ⅓ cup extra-virgin olive oil, 3 tablespoons balsamic vinegar, 1 tablespoon coarse mustard, salt and pepper. Drizzle over the salad. Sprinkle with grated Parmesan.

Preparing Eggplant

- Layer eggplant slices in a colander.

- Sprinkle each layer with a little salt. The salt draws unwanted moisture out of the eggplant.

- Let the eggplant slices drain in the colander over the sink for about 20 minutes.

- Rinse thoroughly, drain well, and pat dry with paper towels.

Blistering Peppers

- Peppers can be roasted in various ways, but roasting them in the oven is fast and easy.

- When peppers roast, their skin puffs up and turns black. It will lift off in whole sections.

- After roasting, allow the peppers to steam for about 15 minutes in a covered bowl or paper bag. This makes it even easier to remove the charred skin.

BASIC RECIPE FOR DOUGH

In Italy, there is no dish more admired than bread

Cheap and simple, bread products play a crucial role in Italian and world cuisine. In most regions of Italy, housewives still make the traditional bread themselves. In the region of Basilicata, the dough is made from wheat flour, yeast, and cooked potatoes. A loaf of this bread is big enough to feed a family for a week.

Ancient Romans used to put small rounds of dough in the oven along with the bread when it was being baked. These rounds, which were similar to focaccia, were offered to the gods in thanks. This custom is still practiced in Calabria, although these by-products of baking are now offered to neighbors instead of the gods.

Yield: makes 2 loaves

Ingredients:

1³/₄ cakes (30 g) fresh yeast or active dry yeast (follow maker's instruction)

1 cup lukewarm water

5 cups bread flour

3 tablespoons virgin olive oil

Pinch salt

Water, as needed

Basic Recipe for Dough

- Dissolve the yeast in the lukewarm water.

- Sift the flour into a large bowl, and make a well in the middle. Add the dissolved yeast, olive oil, a pinch of salt, and enough water (a cup at a time) to enable the mixture to be kneaded into a smooth dough.

- Shape the dough into a ball and let it stand at room temperature, covered loosely with a kitchen towel, until doubled in size, about 1 hour.

- Place the dough in an oiled bowl, and allow it to rise a second time.

Ciabatta: Add more water when making the dough so it is quite wet. On a floured surface, form half the dough into an irregular oval shape about 10 by 4 inches. Place on a greased baking sheet sprinkled with cornmeal. Dimple the loaf with your fingers; drizzle with 1 tablespoon olive oil. Let rise until doubled, then bake at 425°F for 20 to 25 minutes, until deep golden brown.

Filoncino: Divide dough in half. Roll out each half to a 12- by 7-inch rectangle. Starting at the long end, roll up dough. Seal seams and place seam-side down, on a cornmeal-coated baking sheet. Let rise for 1 hour. Preheat oven to 400°F. Place a pan of water on lowest rack. Brush loaves with 1 tablespoon milk; slash their tops in a diagonal pattern. Bake for 25 to 35 minutes, until golden brown.

Sifting Flour

- Sifting flour ensures that you'll be using the correct amount in any dough recipe. It also helps prevents unwanted lumps from forming.

- Making dough in a well is known as the fontana method.

- Into a large bowl, sift the flour, forming a mound. Make a hole in the middle of the mound with your fist.

- Add the liquid to the center of the well. Beat with a fork, gradually bringing the wall of flour into the liquid.

Shaping the Dough

- You can shape the dough with any of several methods.

- Hand-shaping works well for deep-dish pizza.

- Make pizzas and calzones by shaping the dough with a rolling pin.

- For a super-thin crust, you can shape the dough by stretching it with your hands.

PITTA CON POMODORI

Catch the scent of baking bread, and all seems right with the world

This flat, round bread comes from Calabria. It is perfect for panini and can hold lots of goodies without making a mess. These delicious-smelling "bread rings" are by-products of a baking day and are eaten as soon as they come out of the oven. They are salted, brushed with olive oil, or filled with ricotta cheese.

Another well-liked bread is ciabatta, which is made from grade 0 flour—common in Italy but hard to find in the United States. This soft and fairly moist bread has large holes in it, formed during the 6 hours in which the dough is left to rise, giving the bread its characteristic appearance. This aromatic wheat bread with its lightly floured, chewy crust is sold throughout Italy.

Yield: serves 6

Ingredients:

1 pound pitta dough

³/₄ pound ripe tomatoes (preferably tomatoes on the vine)

2 green bell peppers

Extra-virgin olive oil, as needed

6 fresh basil leaves

10 black olives

2 tablespoons capers

Grated Pecorino Romano cheese, as needed

Pitta con Pomodori

- Roll the dough into a round, and place it on an oiled baking sheet.

- Core the tomatoes, and cut them into chunks. Core the peppers, and cut into small chunks. In a sauté pan, heat a little olive oil. Add the tomatoes, peppers, and basil. Cook until the peppers are soft.

- Spread the tomato–pepper mixture, olives, and capers on the dough. Top with grated cheese. Drizzle with olive oil, and bake for 20 to 30 minutes in a preheated 450°F oven.

· · · · RECIPE VARIATION · · · ·

Focaccia: Roll half of the dough into a 10-inch circle. Press the top with your fingers to create dimples. Place on a greased baking sheet. Drizzle dough with 2 tablespoons olive oil and sprinkle with 1 tablespoon each chopped fresh rosemary and chopped fresh oregano; sprinkle on ¼ cup grated Parmesan. Let rise for 1 hour. Bake at 400°F for 16 to 22 minutes, until golden brown.

Coring Tomatoes

- Place each tomato on its side on a cutting board.

- Holding the tomato firmly with one hand, insert a sharp paring knife about an inch outside the core.

- Move the knife back and forth as you rotate the tomato.

- Eventually the core will be cut free and can easily be removed.

Keeping Cheese Fresh

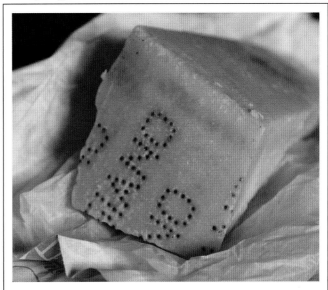

- Once it's cut, cheese is exposed to air and in danger of oxidation, which can cause it to dry out.

- To prevent this, keep wedges of cheese wrapped tightly in plastic.

- Every time you use the wedge of cheese, use new plastic wrap to make sure the seal is always tight.

- Keep grated cheese in a zip-style plastic bag. Store cheese in the warmest part of the refrigerator. Freezing cheese can ruin its texture and flavor.

SAVORY FILLED CROISSANTS

This specialty pastry, stuffed with mouthwatering ingredients, can make any day special

Bread is nothing more than baked dough made from flour and water leavened by yeast. In fact, French bread with its crusty exterior contains only these ingredients and salt. These are called *lean dough products*. Other kinds of bread contain additional ingredients, including sugar, milk, shortening, eggs, and flavoring; they're known as *rich dough products*.

Nonsweet breads contain less sugar but higher amounts of fat so they can be served as dinner rolls. Croissants (the Italian term is *cornetti*) are in this category. To make this dough from scratch, you'll need lots of practice. You can also purchase puff pastry in the frozen-foods section of almost any supermarket. *Yield: serves 4*

Ingredients:

1 sheet frozen puff pastry (half of a 17.3-ounce box)

1 egg

Filling:

6 ounces San Daniele prosciutto, cut into thin strips

4 ounces Parmigiano Reggiano cheese, freshly grated

2–3 tablespoons sour cream

1 tablespoon sharp mustard

Salt and freshly ground pepper

Sweet paprika, as needed

Savory Filled Croissants

- Thaw the pastry, and cut the sheet into quarters. Preheat the oven to 350°F.

- Separate the egg, and beat white and yolk slightly in different bowls.

- In another bowl, combine the filling ingredients, and season with salt, pepper, and paprika to taste.

- Coat and fill the pastries (see technique).

- Rinse a baking sheet under cold water. Set the croissants on the sheet, bending each into a crescent shape. Bake for 20 to 30 minutes, or until golden and crisp.

Mushroom-Filled Croissants: Prepare recipe, but omit filling. Instead, clean and finely chop 3½ ounces small white mushrooms. Cook in 1 tablespoon olive oil until dark golden. Add 1 tablespoon fresh lemon juice, ⅓ cup grated Parmigiano Reggiano cheese, and 2 tablespoons chopped Italian parsley. Season with salt and pepper. Fill croissants with this mixture, then form and bake as directed.

Chocolate-Filled Croissants: Prepare the recipe as directed, but omit the filling. Instead, combine 1 cup semi-sweet chocolate chips, 1 teaspoon cinnamon, and 1 tablespoon powdered sugar in a food processor until finely chopped. Cut the puff pastry into nine squares. Divide the chocolate mixture among the squares, fold over, and glaze with egg wash. Bake as directed.

Quartering Pastry

- Follow the package instructions for thawing the puff pastry.

- With a rolling pin, roll out the pastry slightly into a large square.

- Cut the pastry diagonally into quarters to end up with four triangles.

Coating and Filling the Pastry

- Coat the edges of each puff pastry triangle with beaten egg white (this will be the "glue" that holds the croissant together).

- Spread an equal amount of filling over each puff pastry triangle. Roll up the dough, starting from the straight side of the triangle and moving toward the point.

- Brush the croissant tops with beaten egg yolk. Poke each croissant with a fork so steam can escape while baking.

STUFFED BAGUETTE
This dish requires little effort but is very big on taste

There are as many types of bread as there are regions in Italy. Rustic loaves, corn bread, whole wheat bread, and many other types are available, using a large variety of flour blends.

Bread is eaten in Italy throughout the day. For breakfast, it is dipped in coffee or toasted, bruschetta-style. Bread is also used for cooking; in soups and vegetable dishes; and as an accompaniment to cheeses, sausages, meat dishes, pasta, fresh figs, grapes, and nuts.

The differences in shape are also vast: You can find round flat loaves, tall round loaves, and long bread sticks, in which category the baguette (filoncino) falls. Good filoncino has a crisp crust and lots of holes.

Yield: serves 3

KNACK ITALIAN COOKING

Ingredients:

2 garlic cloves

Fresh basil leaves

¹/₄ cup (¹/₂ stick) soft butter

10 ounces fresh mozzarella cheese

4 medium-size ripe tomatoes (on the vine are best)

Salt and freshly ground pepper

1 baguette

Stuffed Filoncino

- Chop the garlic and basil. Combine with the butter in a small bowl.

- Preheat the oven to 400°F.

- Cut the mozzarella into thin slices. Wash and slice the tomatoes. Season with salt and pepper.

- Cut and stuff the bread (see technique).

- Bake for 15 minutes, or until the cheese is melted.

Pancetta Baguette: Prepare recipe but omit filling. Chop ½ pound pancetta. Cook in 1 tablespoon olive oil with 2 minced shallots until crisp; drain. Mix with 2 cups shredded Fontina, ½ cup grated Parmigiano Reggiano, and ⅓ cup chopped fresh basil leaves. Slice bread into 1-inch slices; do not cut through bottom so slices stay together. Fill with pancetta filling. Bake as directed and serve warm.

Vegetable Baguette: Prepare recipe, omitting filling. Spread garlic and basil butter on each side of bread slices. Chop 2 red bell peppers and slice 1 red onion; sauté in 2 tablespoons olive oil until tender. Remove from heat and cool for 15 minutes. Add 1½ cups grated Asiago cheese. Place mixture in bread. Bake as directed and serve warm.

BREAD

Chopping Garlic and Basil

- Peel and finely chop the garlic. This is easily done by smashing the garlic with the flat side of a large chef's knife. The papery skin will fall off the clove, which you can then mince.

- Cut the basil leaves into thin strips by stacking them, rolling them up, and slicing.

- Mix the garlic and basil with the soft butter to make a compound butter.

Cutting and Stuffing Bread

- Make deep cuts into the loaf of bread at 1-inch intervals. Be careful to not cut all the way through.

- Spread each pocket with some of the compound butter.

- Stuff a slice of mozzarella and a slice of tomato into each pocket.

CALZONES

This dish looks and tastes like a folded pizza—perfect for on-the-go meals

Panini, crostini, and calzone can be served with espresso for a quick lunch or dinner. The filling often reflects the regional ingredients available. Italians love to eat outdoors, and calzones are perfect picnic fare.

Calzones look like folded pizzas and consist of bread dough wrapped around a cheese and vegetable filling. The traditional tomato and garlic calzone can be enhanced with chunks of melting cheese, olives, slices of pepperoni, crumbled bacon, and many other ingredients of your choice.

Another hot calzone combination is a croissant al prosciutto e formaggio. This sandwich combines Italian ham and cheese with a hot buttery-tasting croissant. *Yield: serves 4*

Ingredients:

Filling:

2 tablespoons pure olive oil

1 small red onion, thinly sliced

2 garlic cloves, crushed

1 can (14 ounces) chopped tomatoes

2 ounces sopressata sausage (or sweet Italian sausage with no skin), sliced

$1/2$ cup pitted black olives

7 ounces fresh mozzarella, diced

1 teaspoon dried oregano

Salt and ground black pepper

Prepared calzone dough ("Basic Recipe for Dough" on page 72)

Oregano sprigs, for garnish

Calzones

- Heat oil in frying pan, and sauté onion and garlic for 5 minutes.

- Add tomatoes; cook for 5 more minutes, until slightly reduced. Add the sopressata, olives, mozzarella, and dried oregano.

- Preheat the oven to 400°F.

- Lightly grease two baking sheets.

- Make four calzones.

- Place two calzones on each baking sheet. Bake for 12 to 15 minutes. Cool for 2 minutes, then loosen with a spatula; garnish with oregano sprigs.

Shrimp Calzones: Prepare recipe omitting sausage and olives. Shell and devein 1 cup small fresh shrimp; add to pan with tomatoes; cook until shrimp turn pink. Season with 1 teaspoon dried thyme, salt, and pepper. Let cool 20 minutes. Shape and fill calzones. Brush with 1 teaspoon olive oil and sprinkle with 1 tablespoon grated Parmesan cheese. Place on baking sheets and bake as directed.

Spinach Calzones: Prepare recipe but omit tomatoes, sausage, and olives. Cook onion and garlic in olive oil, then add 1 (10-ounce) package frozen chopped spinach, thawed and drained. Cook for 5 minutes and place in a bowl. Add ⅛ teaspoon nutmeg, 1 cup ricotta cheese, and 1½ cups shredded mozzarella cheese. Fill, shape, and bake the calzones as directed.

Making the Dough

- Make the calzone dough according to "Basic Recipe for Dough."

- Punch down the risen dough and divide it into four portions.

- Roll out each portion of dough into a circle measuring about 8 inches in diameter.

Filling the Calzones

- Spread an equal amount of filling on half of each dough circle, leaving a border around the edge.

- Dampen the edges of the dough circles with cold water.

- Fold the dough circle in half to make a half-moon. Press the edges together to seal tightly.

FOUR-CHEESE CIABATTA BREAD
Few dishes are as satisfying as bread stuffed with four cheeses

This bread is made with bread flour. The method of preparation varies from place to place in Italy, so naturally this dish comes in strong and soft, thin and thick varieties.

The unique flavors of the individual cheeses work harmoniously with the bread. Gorgonzola, a greenish blue cheese, has a spicy, sharp flavor, providing a pleasant contrast to the creamy texture of the cheese. Fontina cheese is dense,

smooth, and slightly elastic. It has a delicate nuttiness with a hint of honey. Parmigiano Reggiano has a sweet and fruity flavor, strong and rich but never overpowering. Pecorino Romano, when it's mature and its characteristic flavor has developed, has a salty and fruity taste that steadily gets stronger as it ages.

Yield: serves 2

Ingredients:

1 loaf ciabatta bread

1 garlic clove, cut in half

2–3 tablespoons olive oil

Filling:

6 tablespoons tomato sauce

1 small red onion, thinly sliced

2 tablespoons chopped pitted olives

2 ounces each of 4 cheeses (Parmigiano Reggiano, Gorgonzola, Fontina, and Pecorino Romano), sliced, grated, or crumbled

Pine nuts, as needed

Salt and black pepper, to taste

Sprigs of basil, for garnish

Four-Cheese Ciabatta Bread

- Preheat the oven to 400°F.

- Prep the ciabatta bread with the garlic and olive oil (see technique).

- Spread the bread with the filling ingredients. Season with salt and pepper.

- Bake for 10 to 12 minutes, or until bubbling and golden brown. Cut into slices; garnish with basil sprigs.

· · · · · · · · GREEN ● LIGHT · · · · · · · · · · · ·

Grating Cheese: To grate cheese, it should be cold. Very soft cheeses will grate more easily if you put them in the freezer for 10 to 15 minutes (no longer). Make sure that the grater has sharp holes. You can coat it with a bit of oil to make cleanup easier. Cut the cheese into manageable pieces and use it immediately after grating so it doesn't dry out.

· · · · · **RECIPE VARIATION** · · · · ·

Pesto Cheese Ciabatta: Prepare the recipe as directed, omitting the topping. Cut the ciabatta in half and spread each half with ½ cup homemade pesto. Sprinkle with ⅓ cup each grated Romano cheese, Parmigiano Reggiano, and part-skim mozzarella. Drizzle each with 1 tablespoon olive oil and sprinkle with pine nuts. Bake as directed until the cheese melts; serve immediately.

Prepping the Ciabatta

- Using a sharp bread knife, split the ciabatta bread in half.

- Rub the cut sides of the ciabatta bread with the cut sides of the garlic cloves.

- Brush the cut sides of the bread with the olive oil. It's now ready to be filled.

Filling the Ciabatta

- The filling consists of layers of flavor, beginning with the tomato sauce. Add the sliced onions and chopped olives.

- Divide the cheeses equally between the ciabatta halves. Sprinkle with pine nuts. Season with salt and pepper.

- The ciabatta bread is now ready for the oven.

PIZZA
Pizza may be the world's favorite food

When I make dough and work it with my hands, not only does it make me proud to continue a tradition followed by many generations before me, but it also relaxes me. There are, however, a few rules that you should follow to produce good dough.

All the ingredients must be at room temperature. The flour should have a high proportion of gluten, which is the protein that makes bread rise, gives it elasticity, and helps it keep its shape once it's baked.

A key ingredient is unbleached all-purpose flour. Semolina, also good for bread, is harder to work with because of its inability to absorb water.

Yield: serves 4

Ingredients:

Pizza dough:

1 package fast-acting yeast

2 cups flour

¼ cup olive oil

½ cup lukewarm water

1 generous pinch salt

Tomato sauce:

1 onion

2 garlic cloves

1 tablespoon olive oil

1 large can (28 ounces) peeled tomatoes

Salt and freshly ground pepper

Choice of toppings:

Sliced mozzarella, basil, pitted olives, anchovies, ham, fresh mushrooms, salami, pepperoni, peppers, onions, goat cheese, grated Pecorino Romano, extra-virgin olive oil for drizzling

Pizza

- In a bowl, mix yeast with flour. Add oil, water, and salt; mix well. Knead dough. Place in bowl; cover with a cloth. Let dough rise for 45 minutes, until it doubles.

- Prepare the tomato sauce.

- Preheat oven to 475°F. Grease a baking sheet.

- Remove dough from bowl and knead on floured surface. Roll out dough to fit baking sheet then transfer to the sheet, folding edges over to make a crust.

- Spread tomato sauce over dough; add toppings. Bake for 20 minutes, until cheese melts and crust is golden.

Sausage Pizza: Prepare the dough as directed and top with tomato sauce. Slice 4 ounces sopressata (hard salami) into very thin slices and arrange on the tomato sauce. Top with 1½ cups grated part-skim mozzarella and ¼ cup grated Romano. Bake as directed, let stand 5 minutes, then slice into wedges to serve.

Seafood Pizza: Prepare the dough as directed and top with tomato sauce. In a medium bowl, combine ¼ pound cooked shrimp, 10 ounces canned baby clams, well drained, and ⅓ cup minced Italian parsley. Arrange over the tomato sauce; sprinkle with 1 cup shredded Fontina and ⅓ cup grated Parmesan. Bake as directed.

Layers of Flavor

Making the Sauce

- The freshly made tomato sauce will be the first layer of flavor placed on the pizza dough.

- Personal preference will dictate what toppings come next. Some of the possibilities include a three-cheese pizza and a meat lover's special. For a healthier version, add mushrooms, peppers, and onions.

- Always top off your pizza with a drizzle of extra-virgin olive oil.

- To make the tomato sauce, peel the onion and garlic; chop finely.

- In a skillet, heat the olive oil over medium heat; sauté the onion and garlic until translucent. Chop the tomatoes into small pieces, and stir into the skillet.

- Let the sauce simmer gently, uncovered, for 5 minutes, or until slightly thickened. Season to taste with salt and pepper.

PIZZA WITH SQUASH & BACON

This is a delicious way to introduce your palate to something new and original

Gennaro Lombardi, an immigrant from southern Italy, opened the first pizzeria in New York in 1905, and this round dough, topped with delicious ingredients, became an overnight success. Soon after, other "pizzaioli" followed, making pizza one of the most successful dishes ever invented. Research suggests that pizza is even more popular than hamburgers.

This recipe calls for squash as a topping on pizza. Autumn is squash season. Outdoor markets brim with baskets full of squashes in an array of colors. Coupled with the smoky flavor of bacon, winter squash adds beautiful color, substantial body, and sweet flavor to this pizza dish.
Yield: serves 6 (Makes two 9-inch pizzas)

Ingredients:

Toppings:

¹/₄ small butternut squash, seeded, peeled, and cut into thin slices

2 tablespoons olive oil, divided

Salt and ground pepper

¹/₄ pound hickory-smoked bacon, diced small

3 ounces mozzarella cheese, shredded

3 ounces smoked mozzarella cheese, shredded

Pizza dough (see recipe on page 84)

¹/₄ cup chopped fresh sage

Pizza with Squash and Bacon

- Position a rack in the bottom third of the oven, and place a pizza stone on it.

- Prep and cook the squash.

- Add 1 tablespoon of oil to a frying pan over medium heat. Add bacon and cook, stirring, until it turns golden, about 5 minutes;

drain on paper towels. In a bowl, toss the two mozzarella cheeses.

- Shape dough, and top with cheese, bacon, and sage.

- Slide pizza directly onto the stone. Bake until golden and crisp, 8 to 10 minutes. Repeat for second pizza.

Two-Bacon Pizza: Prepare the recipe as directed, omitting the butternut squash. Add ¼ pound smoked pancetta, diced, to the diced bacon and cook until crisp. Drain on paper towels. Assemble the pizza as directed, using all part-skim mozzarella cheese. Top with 2 sliced red tomatoes and sprinkle with 1 teaspoon dried oregano. Bake as directed.

ZOOM

About Bacon: Pancetta is the Italian version of bacon, but it is usually unsmoked. Bacon comes in presliced, unsliced, and thick-sliced varieties, flavored with everything from apples to peppercorns. Sauté it over medium heat, stirring frequently with a spoon, until it's crisp and golden brown. Remove from the pan using a slotted spoon and drain on paper towels before using.

Prepping and Cooking Squash

Shaping and Topping Dough

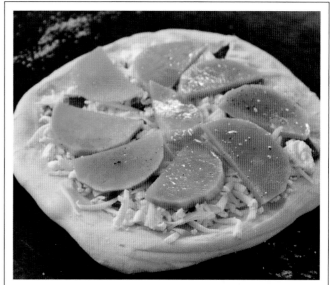

PIZZA

- Preheat the oven to 500°F. Bring a large saucepan three-quarters full of salted water to a boil. Add squash slices, and boil for about 3 minutes.

- Using a slotted spoon, transfer the squash to paper towels and drain well. In a large frying pan, over high heat, warm 1 tablespoon of oil.

- Add the squash and cook, turning often, until golden on the edges and cooked through, about 5 minutes. Season generously with salt and pepper. Remove the squash and let cool.

- Punch down the dough, and turn it out onto a floured work surface, Divide the dough in half; roll out each half into a circle 9 inches in diameter and ¼ inch thick.

- Transfer one pizza at a time to a well-floured pizza baking sheet. Sprinkle the two with equal amounts of the cheese, bacon, and sage. Top with half of the squash slices.

CHICKEN PIADINE W/BABY SPINACH

This is a delicious way to make your children happy and healthy

Piadine (the name means "little pizza") are actually unleavened, thin breads traditionally cooked on a stovetop. For the sake of convenience, the cooking style has evolved from the top of the stove into the oven. If you have any leftover dough in the freezer, you can use it for this recipe. You can assemble piadine with any manner of ingredients. For the dough, use the Pizza recipe on page 84.

Pizza tastes better when baked in a wood-fired stone oven; only this way can the needed high temperature of 750°F be reached. Pizza is ready when the edges curl and turn golden brown, the base is crisp, and the cheese has melted.
Yield: serves 6

Ingredients:

Pizza dough (recipe on page 84)

All-purpose flour, as needed for dusting work surface

2¼ cups roasted, peeled, and seeded red bell peppers (store-bought is fine), divided

3 tablespoons roasted garlic paste (available in most supermarkets)

Salt and freshly ground pepper, to taste

⅓ cup freshly grated Parmigiano Reggiano cheese

3 tablespoons finely chopped fresh oregano

Coarse cornmeal, as needed for sprinkling on baking sheets

About ¼ cup Whole Citrus Vinaigrette (see below)

9 cups loosely packed baby spinach

1½ cups diced fresh mozzarella cheese (½-inch cubes)

3 chicken breast halves, cooked, boned, and torn into shreds

Whole Citrus Vinaigrette:

2 lemons

½ navel orange

1 shallot

1½ cups olive oil

1 teaspoon salt

½ teaspoon freshly ground pepper

Chicken Piadine with Baby Spinach

- Divide dough into 6 balls; dust tops with flour, cover with towel; let rise 15 minutes.

- Puree 1½ cups roasted peppers with garlic paste, salt, and pepper. Cut remaining peppers into long, narrow strips. Set aside.

- Roll each ball into a circle 8 or 9 inches and ⅛ inch thick. Spread with 3 tablespoons of puree. Sprinkle with 1 tablespoon of cheese and 1½ teaspoons oregano.

- Bake pizzas. Let crusts cool. Prepare dressing and salad. Transfer crusts to plates, and top each with salad.

Piadine with Prosciutto: Make the dough and shape as directed. Omit chicken and roasted red bell peppers. Spread dough with roasted garlic paste and sprinkle with salt and pepper. Bake as directed. Combine the baby spinach, vinaigrette, 1 cup crumbled Gorgonzola cheese, and ½ pound thinly sliced prosciutto. Top pizza and serve.

Pesto Tomato Piadine: Prepare recipe except omit vinaigrette and chicken breasts. Make a dressing by combining ½ cup homemade pesto with 2 tablespoons balsamic vinegar and 2 tablespoons plain yogurt in a large bowl; whisk until smooth. Add 4 cups arugula leaves, 1½ cups diced smoked mozzarella, 2 cups baby spinach, and 3 tomatoes, chopped. Top pizza with mixture.

Whole Citrus Vinaigrette

Baking the Piadine

- Juice the lemons, orange, and shallot in a juice extractor. Or squeeze the citrus by hand and use a garlic press for the shallot; if you're using this method, double the ingredients. Put the juice in a bowl and slowly whisk in the olive oil.

- Season with salt and pepper to taste. Refrigerate for up to 3 days.

- In a large bowl, toss together the vinaigrette, spinach, mozzarella, reserved pepper strips, and chicken. Taste for seasoning.

- Place two baking sheets in 500°F preheated oven.

- Remove the baking sheets from the hot oven. Sprinkle the sheets evenly with cornmeal (which keeps the pizza from sticking). Transfer the pizza rounds to the sheets.

- Bake until slightly underdone, about 8 to 12 minutes. Carefully remove the baking sheets from the oven.

GRILLED EGGPLANT PIZZA
This is a wonderful and classic Italian option for vegetarians

This is what's called a "dry" pizza, meaning it has no tomato sauce. I like the flavor of buffalo mozzarella on this dish, but any fresh mozzarella will do. Provolone is also a good choice. You will find it to be more convenient to grill one or two larger pies rather than six individual pizzas.

Eggplant is one of the most versatile vegetables. The flavor of the eggplant changes depending on the method of cooking. It's a good substitute for meat. When in season, eggplants do not need to be peeled or salted and are delicious when grilled. Sprinkle with a drizzle of extra-virgin olive oil, flavored with a splash of fresh garlic. You can also add eggplant to panini, or serve it as a side dish.

Yield: serves 6

KNACK ITALIAN COOKING

Ingredients:

Piadine dough (recipe on page 84)

All-purpose flour, as needed for dusting work surface

Extra-virgin olive oil, as needed for brushing on veggies, plus about $1/4$ cup

1 tablespoon minced garlic

2 tablespoons finely chopped fresh oregano

1 tablespoon red pepper flakes (optional)

3 eggplants, about 3 pounds total, sliced $3/4$ inch thick

Freshly ground pepper

2 large yellow or red bell peppers

1 cup pitted kalamata olives

$1/2$ pound buffalo mozzarella cheese or provolone cheese, coarsely shredded

3 cups packed arugula

Balsamic vinegar, as needed

Grilled Eggplant Pizza

- Divide dough to make six round pizzas. Prepare grill.

- Brush each dough round with 1 teaspoon olive oil. Place on grill, oiled-side up, and cook about 2 minutes. Turn and brush each round with another teaspoon of oil. Sprinkle each with one-sixth of the garlic, oregano, red pepper flakes, eggplant, bell peppers, olives, and cheese. Cover grill; cook until rounds are browned on bottom and cheese has melted, about 7 minutes.

- Transfer to plates, and top each with an equal amount of arugula. Sprinkle lightly with vinegar.

Oven Pizza: To bake the pizza in the oven, position a rack on the lowest rungs. Place two large baking sheets on the rack and preheat to 500°F. Remove the sheets, dust them with cornmeal, and transfer the dough round to them. Brush each round with about 1 teaspoon olive oil. Scatter the ingredients evenly over the rounds. Bake until the crust is light brown on the bottom, 8 to 12 minutes.

Grilled Mushroom Pizza: Prepare recipe omitting eggplant and arugula. Slice 8 ounces each cremini and white button mushrooms. Place in a grill basket; grill over medium coals until golden. Remove from heat and toss with garlic, oregano, and red pepper flakes. Grill dough on one side; turn and top with mushroom mixture, olives, and cheese; grill until the cheese melts. Drizzle with vinegar.

Prepare Veggies for Grilling

- Prepare the grill.

- Salt the eggplant, and set aside for 30 minutes; rinse and pat dry. Brush the eggplant with oil and season with pepper.

- Toss the peppers with oil.

- Toss both on the grill, and cook the eggplant until brown on the first side. Do not disturb the veggies for 3 minutes.

Dividing the Dough

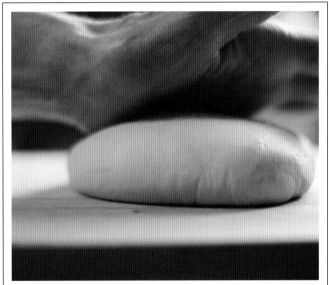

- Divide the dough into six equal balls. Working on a flour-free surface, roll each ball under the palm of your hand. As it rolls, it will stick slightly to the surface.

- Dust the work surface lightly with flour. Pat down

each ball lightly, dust the top with flour, cover with a towel, and let rise for about 15 minutes.

- With a rolling pin, roll out each ball into a circle 8 or 9 inches in diameter and about 1/8 inch thick.

PIZZA

NEAPOLITAN PIZZA

The classic pizza Napoletana requires few ingredients and very little work to get amazing results

In 1858 a chef by the name of Emanuele Rocco came up with this tasty treat totally by accident. One day while making bread, Emanuele found himself with a small leftover piece of dough. Not exactly sure what to do with it, he playfully shaped it into a circle, topped it with tomatoes, mozzarella, anchovies, and capers (just a few things he had lying around the kitchen), and baked it in the oven until golden brown.

The aroma permeated throughout the surrounding areas, making passersby curious about the origin of the delectable smell and, consequently, looking for a sample. The news of this delicacy spread like wildfire throughout Italy, and the rest is history. Enjoy. *Yield: serves 4*

Ingredients:

Pizza dough (recipe on page 84)

1 can (24–30 ounces) plum tomatoes, sliced

$^1/_2$ pound buffalo mozzarella, divided

1 can or 1 small bottle anchovies in oil

Generous pinch oregano

Fresh basil, as needed

Extra-virgin olive oil, as needed

Neapolitan Pizza

- Make pizza dough. The dough should be stretched thin in the middle and thicker at the edges, in a large round pizza pan (9 to 12 inches wide).

- Preheat the oven to 400°F.

- Top the dough with the tomatoes, half of the mozzarella, anchovies, oregano, and basil.

- Bake for 15 to 20 minutes, or until the edges are golden brown. Top the pizza with the remaining mozzarella and return it to the oven for 1 to 2 minutes.

Spreading Dough

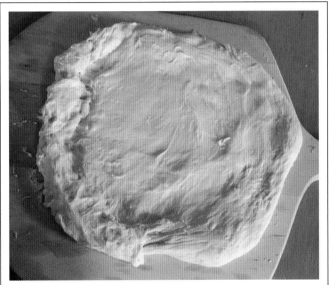

- To make a thin-crust pizza, knead a ball of dough for about 1 minute. On a lightly floured work surface, shape the dough into a disk about 1 inch thick.

- Starting from the center of the dough, press it out with the heels of your hands. Work around the dough to achieve the desired shape, usually a circle.

- Dust with flour whenever needed to prevent sticking.

Adding the Toppings

- Spread the sliced tomatoes on the shaped pizza dough.

- Spread half of the mozzarella, cut into medium-thick slices.

- Spread the anchovies evenly over the dough. Sprinkle the oregano and basil over the entire surface.

- Drizzle the olive oil lightly over the pizza for the finishing touch.

PIZZA

PIZZA WITH CLAMS

Incorporating fish in pizza is one of the most delicious ways to serve it

The ancient Romans were already familiar with pizza even though the dish they enjoyed hardly resembled the one we love so much. They sometimes folded the dough in half, too, making what we now call calzones.

Some of the best dishes I have eaten have been in little out-of-the-way places in Italy, where I first tasted this particular pizza (pizza alle vongole in Italian). It left a great impression on me. Italian chefs and cooks understand that the simple treatment of clams is best. The ways to cook seafood are almost endless; incorporating it into pizza is one of the most delicious.

Yield: serves 2

KNACK ITALIAN COOKING

Ingredients:

Pizza dough (recipe on page 84)

3 very ripe tomatoes

2 pounds clams (canned)

¼ cup extra-virgin olive oil

1 garlic clove, chopped

1 small bunch parsley, chopped

1 teaspoon oregano

Freshly ground pepper

Pizza with Clams

- Follow the directions on how to make and shape pizza dough as shown on page 93.

- Preheat the oven to 400°F.

- Skin, seed, and dice the tomatoes. Arrange the tomatoes on top of the prepared pizza dough.

- Bake for 15 to 20 minutes.

- Prepare the clams (see technique). Keep them warm until the pizza is done. Top the pizza with the clams. Season with oregano and pepper to taste.

White Pizza with Clams: Prepare the recipe as directed, except omit the tomatoes. Add ¼ pound diced, cooked pancetta, 2 pounds clams, and 2 cups shredded mozzarella cheese on the pizza; top with the garlic, parsley, and oregano. Bake as directed. Sprinkle with 2 teaspoons minced fresh rosemary and 2 tablespoons chopped Italian parsley; serve immediately.

Pizza with Fresh Clams: Prepare recipe omitting the canned clams. Instead, use 3 pounds fresh clams in the shell. Scrub well, then rinse in water. Discard any clams that do not close tightly. Heat 2 tablespoons olive oil in a skillet; add clams and 3 minced garlic cloves. Cook until clams open, about 5 minutes. Discard any that remain closed. Remove clams from their shells and use on the pizza.

Preparing the Tomatoes

Sautéing the Clams

PIZZA

- Drop the tomatoes into a pot of boiling water for 1 to 2 minutes. Use a slotted spoon to remove them from the pot. The skin will now come off very easily.

- Cut the tomatoes in half, and place them cut-side down on paper towels to

drain. After a few minutes, inspect each tomato half. Use a teaspoon to scrape out any stubborn seeds.

- On a cutting board with a very sharp knife, cut the tomatoes into small, medium, or large dice.

- In a large frying pan over medium-high heat, warm the olive oil. Add the garlic and parsley; cook for 3 to 4 minutes, stirring often and being careful to not burn the garlic.

- Drain the canned clams. Add the clams to the frying pan and cook for 1 more minute, or until the clams are heated through.

ROTELLE SALAD W/GRILLED VEGGIES
This simple recipe is perfect for a warm summer afternoon

Dry pasta is made from *durum semolina* flour, a "strong flour" that results in a chewy bite—that al dente sensation. It's best to buy good-quality pasta so you don't have to worry, about limp pasta even when you overcook it. Pasta should not be rinsed after it's cooked (except when used for pasta salad). Doing so rinses away the starch that is necessary for the pasta and sauce to cling together. This combination gives you a generous portion of sauce on each forkful of pasta.

Barilla is one of the oldest brands of fresh and dry pasta. Pietro Barilla opened his first store in 1877 in the center of Parma where he sold fresh pasta all'uovo (fresh egg pasta) and pasta secca (dry pasta).

Yield: serves 8

Ingredients:

Salad:

1 large red pepper, chopped

¹/₄ pound whole small mushrooms

¹/₄ pound green beans, steamed

¹/₄ pound wax beans, steamed

1 medium zucchini, cubed

2 carrots, sliced and parboiled

1 pound dry rotelle

Marinade:

1 cup olive oil

¹/₂ cup white wine vinegar

2 teaspoons prepared mustard

2 teaspoons dried tarragon

2 tablespoons dried basil

2 teaspoons dried thyme

Salt and pepper, to taste

Rotelle Salad with Grilled Vegetables

- Grill vegetables for salad and put them in a large bowl. Combine all the ingredients for the marinade in a large jar and shake well.

- Toss the marinade and vegetables together. Cover the bowl with plastic wrap and refrigerate for 24 hours, stirring occasionally.

- Several hours before serving the pasta salad, cook and combine the rotelle with the vegetables and marinade.

- Refrigerate the salad until half an hour before serving time, tossing it periodically. Let it come to room temperature before serving.

• • • • RECIPE VARIATION • • • •

Chicken Rotelle Salad: Divide the marinade in half. Add 4 boneless, skinless chicken breasts to half of marinade and refrigerate. Grill the vegetables and add them to remaining marinade; refrigerate. The next day, grill the chicken for 15 to 20 minutes, until done, then slice. Bring chicken marinade to a boil; boil 2 minutes; combine with chicken. Cook pasta, then toss everything together with ½ cup grated Parmesan cheese. Chill.

Grilling Vegetables

Cooking Pasta for Salads

- Prepare a medium-hot fire in the grill. Lightly oil the grill rack. Use a vegetable grill rack, if available.

- In a large bowl, combine the red peppers, mushrooms, green beans, wax beans, zucchini, and carrot slices. Add 2 tablespoons of olive oil. If desired, you can also add 1 teaspoon crushed fresh rosemary and 2 whole garlic cloves for added flavor. Toss well to coat the vegetables with oil.

- Grill the vegetables, turning them often, until lightly charred, approximately 5 minutes.

- Cook the pasta according to the directions on the package.

- Drain the pasta and rinse it under cold running water. (Pasta usually isn't rinsed, unless it's being used in a salad.) Drain well.

- Combine the cooked pasta with the rest of the salad ingredients.

DRY PASTA

97

PASTA PRIMAVERA
A sea of spring colors

Pasta Primavera contains only fresh vegetables, seasoned with herbs, lightly salted and peppered. The most common mistake people make with this dish is failing to sauté the vegetable long enough to concentrate their flavors. The rule is to choose a combination of different textures, colors, and flavors. Here is a suggested combination for each season and the order in which to cook them.

Spring combination: Yellow squash, red peppers, asparagus, peas. Summer combination: Courgettes, sweet corn, okra, tomatoes. Autumn combination: Broccoli, cauliflower, wild mushrooms. Winter combination: Cauliflower, shallots, spinach, avocado.
Yield: serves 4

Ingredients:

3 cups assorted vegetables (see suggestions above)

Olive oil, as needed

Salt and pepper, to taste

1 pound pasta, cooked

Parmigiano Reggiano cheese, shaved as needed

Pasta Primavera

- Sauté the vegetables in olive oil, adding the slowest-cooking ingredients first.

- Cover the pan for a few minutes to speed up the cooking process.

- Or you can sauté each vegetable by itself in a frying pan. Place each batch of cooked vegetables in a large bowl. Season with salt and pepper.

- Serve the cooked vegetables over the cooked pasta; linguine or fettuccine is recommended. Top with shavings of Parmigiano Reggiano.

Summer Pasta Primavera: Prepare recipe as directed, but use 2 cups fresh green beans, 3 ears of sweet corn with the kernels cut off, 1 red and 1 yellow bell pepper, 1 yellow summer squash, cut into slices, and 3 red ripe tomatoes, diced. Cook the beans first; then add the peppers and squash, and finally the corn. Add the tomatoes when you mix the vegetables with the pasta; top with ½ cup torn basil leaves.

Farfalle Primavera: Prepare recipe as directed, except cook 1 sweet red onion, sliced, with 3 cloves minced garlic in 2 tablespoons olive oil. Add 1 sliced zucchini, and 2 sliced orange bell peppers; cook until tender, about 5 minutes. Cook 1 pound dry farfalle pasta until al dente; drain, reserving ½ cup pasta water. Toss the pasta with the vegetables, reserved water, and ½ cup grated Parmesan cheese; serve.

Spring Vegetables

The Right Size

- Spring is certainly an appropriate time to make Pasta Primavera.

- You can use almost any kind of vegetable, although Italians prefer the crispness of broccoli, carrots, peas, onions, and bell peppers, both red and green.

- Roasting the vegetables in the oven will result in even more flavor.

- This dish is usually served warm, but a chilled Pasta Primavera is a nice addition to the summer table.

- Pasta Primavera can also be made with pasta that comes in small shapes, including farfalle (or bowtie), penne, and fusilli.

- All the vegetables in this dish should be of uniform size, slightly smaller than the pasta used.

- If you use a long pasta such as spaghetti or fettuccine, slice the vegetables into thin strips similar to the shape of the pasta.

DRY PASTA

SPAGHETTI CARBONARA

This sauce of bacon, cheese, and eggs is perfect with long thin pasta

Many Italian pasta dishes were inspired by necessity. This very tasty and elegant dish is the result of coal mine workers' need to survive poverty, hence the name carbonara, which means "charcoal-style" in Italian.

The correct combination of pasta and sauce is almost a science in itself. There are a few simple rules to follow when picking out the pasta. Filled pasta, like ravioli, has lots of flavor on its own, so the only sauce needed is a sage butter, a light tomato, or sometimes a cream. Thin pasta fresca (fresh pasta) needs only a few shavings of truffle with butter and/or some shaved Parmigiano. Heavy pasta fresca, like tagliatelle, on the other hand, needs a strong sauce. *Yield: serves 2*

Ingredients:

3 ounces pancetta or bacon

1 tablespoon olive oil

8 ounces dry spaghetti

2 eggs

2 tablespoons light cream

$^1/_3$ cup grated Parmigiano Reggiano cheese

Salt and pepper, to taste

Spaghetti Carbonara

- Render the pancetta or bacon in oil in a frying pan.

- Cook the spaghetti according to package directions. Beat the eggs in a bowl; mix in the cream and cheese. Season with salt and pepper to taste.

- When the spaghetti is al dente, drain it and place in a large bowl (do not rinse). Immediately pour the egg mixture over the hot pasta, tossing thoroughly. The eggs are cooked by the heat of the pasta.

- After adding the egg mixture, toss in the pancetta or bacon, and serve.

Carbonara with Peas: Prepare recipe but cook the bacon until crisp and drain. Pour off bacon fat but do not wipe pan. Add 1 chopped onion and 2 minced garlic cloves to pan; cook for 4 minutes, until tender. Remove from heat and add 2 cups frozen baby peas; set aside. Continue with recipe as directed. When egg mixture is tossed with the pasta, add pea mixture, bacon, and cheese, toss. Serve.

Rich Carbonara: Prepare recipe except cook 2 minced shallots in the bacon fat. Remove the pan from the heat and top with 2 cups chopped baby spinach; cover and set aside. Beat 3 egg yolks with ½ cup heavy cream, cheese, salt, and pepper. Toss the cooked pasta with the egg yolk mixture; add the spinach mixture and toss. Serve immediately.

Grate Your Own Cheese

- Freshly grated Parmigiano Reggiano cheese is the most flavorful and aromatic.

- Italians always buy Parmigiano Reggiano by the wedge so they can grate their own when needed. It may be more work, but it's definitely worth it.

- Pre-grated cheese loses its flavor quickly because more surface area is exposed to air. To guarantee the finest results, buy cheese by the wedge, and grate your own.

Rendering

- Dice the pancetta or bacon into small pieces.

- Heat the olive oil in a frying pan. Add the diced meat.

- Cook the meat until the fat is transparent. Use a slotted spoon to remove the cooked meat from the pan, and set it on a paper towel to drain.

DRY PASTA

FARFALLE ARRABBIATA

This spicy recipe is just perfect for people who like a bit of heat in their lives

Farfalla is Italian for "butterfly." The name for this particular type of pasta is derived from its shape; it resembles a butterfly or, to some eyes, a bowtie.

Dry pasta (pasta secca) does not have much flavor by itself; it needs the accompaniment of strong sauces to shine.

The rule is that the bigger the space inside the pasta, the more sauce it can absorb. For pasta to cook correctly, you need 4 cups of water and ½ teaspoon of salt for every 4 ounces of pasta. Pasta has to have room to move while cooking so it won't stick together. Before adding pasta, water must be brought to a fast boil, and you should maintain the boiling throughout the cooking process. *Yield: serves 4–6*

Ingredients:

2 tablespoons olive oil

¹/₂ cup thinly sliced onion

2 garlic cloves, chopped

1 teaspoon crushed red pepper flakes

1 cup diced prosciutto (about ¹/₄ pound)

2 (28-ounce) cans plum tomatoes

¹/₃ cup fresh basil

1 tablespoon chopped fresh oregano or mint

Salt and freshly ground black pepper, to taste

1 cup frozen peas

1 pound farfalle (bowtie pasta)

Grated Pecorino Romano cheese, as needed

Farfalle Arrabbiata

- In a saucepan, heat the olive oil. Add onion and sauté until soft. Add garlic and crushed red pepper flakes. Sauté until garlic is soft but not brown.

- Add the prosciutto. Add tomatoes, breaking them up with a wooden spoon; stir well and simmer for 5 minutes. Add seasonings.

- Stir well and simmer for 20 minutes, covered, over medium heat. Add the peas and cook 5 minutes more.

- Cook the farfalle. Drain. Place in bowl, add hot sauce, and toss well to coat. Serve with grated cheese.

102

Pasta Arrabiate with Shrimp: Prepare recipe except prepare 1 pound medium shrimp by deveining and removing the shells. Omit the prosciutto. Add the shrimp and ½ cup light cream to the tomato sauce along with the frozen peas; cook until the shrimp curl and turn pink. Cook the pasta and toss with the sauce mixture; sprinkle with cheese and serve immediately.

ZOOM

Cooking Pasta: Since pasta is made of flour, water, and eggs, it must be seasoned when cooked. Always salt the cooking water. Italians say that the water should be "as salty as the sea." The salt brings out the nutty flavor of the pasta and helps it keep its firm texture. Pasta should be cooked al dente, which means "to the tooth." It should still be slightly firm in the center.

Sautéing Prosciutto

- With a very sharp knife, cut the prosciutto into a small dice, approximately ½ inch in size.

- Add the diced prosciutto to the saucepan over medium-high heat. Stirring often, sauté the prosciutto until it begins to render, or let go of, its fat.

Cooking Farfalle

- In a large pot, bring 4 to 6 quarts of water to a rolling boil. Add salt.

- Add the farfalle to the boiling water. Stir gently. Return to a boil.

- For authentic al dente pasta, boil uncovered, stirring occasionally, for 11 to 12 minutes. For more tender pasta, boil an additional minute or two. Test for doneness by tasting the pasta, using a slotted spoon to lift it out of the water.

- Remove the pot from the heat. Drain well, and serve as desired.

DRY PASTA

RIGATONI WITH DRIED TOMATOES

A ragu is a sauce in which meat, tomatoes, and sometimes other vegetables are simmered together slowly

In southern Italy, ripe plum tomatoes are dried on long wooden boards in the hot Mediterranean sun until ready to be packed in olive oil. They are perfect to use in salads, in antipasti and sauces, or for a fast delicious meal, when hungry family and friends drop by unexpectedly.

Rigatoni absorbs and supports strong sauces. Rigatoni, ziti, and penne adapt well to baked pasta dishes and remain evenly distributed throughout the sauce while baking. Pasta made from durum semolina does best in pasta salads because it stays firm, even when left in dressing for long periods of time. Fresh pasta, on the other hand, absorbs too much liquid and becomes soggy quickly. *Yield: serves 6*

Ingredients:

1 cup dried tomatoes packed in olive oil (homemade or store-bought), drained, with oil reserved

1 garlic clove, minced

1 pound rigatoni

3 tablespoons minced basil

¹/₂ cup grated Parmigiano Reggiano cheese

¹/₂ cup grated Asiago cheese

Rigatoni with Dried Tomatoes

- Place the tomatoes in saucepan, stir in the garlic, and cook for 3 to 5 minutes over medium heat. Remove from the heat and set aside.

- In a large pot of boiling water, cook the rigatoni until al dente. Drain, reserving ⅓ cup of cooking water.

- Place the rigatoni in a serving bowl and add the tomato mixture, reserved cooking water, and basil. Toss to coat well. Add cheese, and toss again.

Rigatoni with Sausage and Tomatoes: Prepare recipe except cook 1 pound sweet or hot Italian sausage with 1 chopped onion in a skillet. Drain; add tomatoes with their oil and garlic; cook 45 minutes, until tomatoes plump. Cook pasta until al dente; drain; reserve ½ cup cooking water. Combine pasta with sausage mixture, reserved water, and basil and toss. Add cheese, toss again, and serve.

Rigatoni with Fresh Tomatoes: Prepare recipe but use 4 red ripe tomatoes. Cut the tomatoes in half and remove the seeds with your finger. Cut into ½-inch dice. Cook 1 chopped onion in 3 tablespoons olive oil; add garlic and tomatoes. Season with salt and pepper and simmer for 10 minutes. Cook pasta; drain, reserving pasta water, and proceed with recipe.

Drying Tomatoes

- You can purchase sun-dried tomatoes, which are expensive, or you can dry your own.

- Core the tomatoes and cut them in half lengthwise. Place them cut-side down on a wire rack over a baking sheet in a preheated 225°F

oven. Bake the tomatoes until they have the texture of dried fruit. This may take a day or longer, depending on their size.

- Or you can purchase a dehydrator, and dry tomatoes according to the manufacturer's directions.

Blending Ingredients

- Drain the dried tomatoes, reserving 2 tablespoons of their oil.

- Place the tomatoes and the reserved oil in a blender or processor, and pulse until coarsely ground.

- This tomato mixture combined with the reserved cooking water and basil is the sauce for the rigatoni.

PASTA W/SHRIMP & LEMON SAUCE

Gentle cooking methods like steaming, poaching, and light broiling are the best

This meal has the added advantage of using store-bought pasta secca while still looking very elegant. The sauce takes only minutes to prepare, leaving you plenty of time to enjoy your family and friends. Seafood is extremely popular in Italy, and it's hardly a surprise that there is such variety.

Seafood is divided into four main groups: crustaceans (shrimp and crabs); shellfish (mussels, clams, and scallops); limpets and murex shells; squid, cuttlefish, and octopus.

These types are very different, but they have one thing in common: They are best eaten fresh. They do not need any elaborate flavorings; leaving them simple helps you fully appreciate the tangy freshness of the sea. *Yield: serves 4*

Ingredients:

1 teaspoon butter

4 green onions, chopped

Salt, to taste

1 pound linguine

8 ounces peeled and cooked shrimp

Sauce:

1 cup heavy cream

$\frac{1}{2}$ cup vegetable stock (low-sodium)

2–3 tablespoons fresh lemon juice

4 leaves fresh basil, shredded

Freshly ground pepper

Pasta with Shrimp and Lemon Sauce

- Melt the butter in a large skillet over medium heat, and sauté the green onions until softened.

- In a large pot, bring 5 quarts water and 2 tablespoons salt to a boil. Cook the linguine until al dente. Taste it to test after 7 to 8 minutes.

- Make the sauce (see technique). Just before serving, add the cooked shrimp to the sauce.

- Drain linguine and pour it directly into the skillet with the sauce. Toss well.

GREEN ● LIGHT

Pasta Cooking Tips: When you are preparing a pasta that is going to finish cooking in a sauce, make sure to leave it undercooked a bit. Test the pasta a couple of minutes before it is supposed to be done according to the package directions. There should be a small bit of white uncooked pasta in the center. The pasta will cook through in the sauce and absorb some of its flavors.

·· · · RECIPE VARIATION · · · ·

Linguine with Chicken: Prepare the recipe as directed, omitting the green onions and shrimp. Chop 1 large yellow onion and 3 garlic cloves. Cook in 2 tablespoons olive oil and 1 tablespoon butter for 5 minutes. Add 3 cubed boneless, skinless chicken breasts; sprinkle with salt and pepper. Cook until the chicken is just done, about 8 to 10 minutes. Proceed with the recipe as directed.

Cutting Onions

Making the Sauce

- Rinse the green onions under cold running water.

- With a sharp knife, cut off the root ends. Remove any wilted green parts.

- Line the onions up in a neat row. With a large knife, chop them into the desired lengths.

- A rough chop will result in onion pieces about ½ inch long. A fine chop will result in very fine pieces.

- In a skillet over medium heat, combine the cream, vegetable stock, lemon juice, and basil.

- Bring to a simmer, stirring constantly. Do not allow to boil.

- Continue to simmer. The mixture will gradually reduce, resulting in a creamy sauce. Taste the sauce, and season with salt and pepper.

DRY PASTA

CLASSIC EGG PASTA

Dough for pasta all'uovo should feel as silky as your finest lingerie

When making pasta dough, bring all the ingredients to room temperature before mixing so they easily combine and produce a smooth dough.

Combination 1 is standard for most kind of fresh pasta:
2⅓ cups all-purpose flour
3 eggs
1 tablespoon olive oil

½ teaspoon salt
1 tablespoon water, if required
Combination 2 stays firm when cooked:
1 cup finely ground semolina for pasta
1 cup all-purpose flour
2 eggs + 1 egg yolk
½ teaspoon salt

Ingredients:

3 cups all-purpose flour

4 eggs

1 teaspoon salt (optional)

1 tablespoon olive oil (optional)

Classic Egg Pasta

- To mix the dough with a fork, start by sifting the flour into a mound on a flat, smooth work surface. With your fingers, make a well in the middle.

- Crack open the eggs into the well; add the salt and oil. Beat the mixture with a fork, gradually combining it with the surrounding flour.

- Continue until all of the flour and eggs have been incorporated into a ball of dough. Knead and shape the dough.

Combination 3 for stuffed pasta, like ravioli and tortellini:
2⅓ cups all-purpose flour
2 eggs + 4 egg yolks
½ teaspoon salt
Combination 4 is a rich dough, ideal for tagliatelle/fettuccine:
2⅓ cups all-purpose flour
1 egg
7 egg yolks
1 tablespoon olive oil
½ teaspoon salt   *Yield: serves 4*

MAKE IT EASY

Rolling pasta is an art. You can roll by hand or use a pasta machine. Be sure that the pasta dough rests for at least 30 minutes before rolling so the gluten has a chance to relax and the dough can be rolled. Follow the directions that come with your pasta machine, gradually decreasing the thickness of the pasta each time it passes through the machine.

Mixing Dough by Hand

- With your fingers, make a well in center of flour (it should resemble a volcano).

- Pour eggs into well along with salt and oil. Using a large fork, stir the flour into wet ingredients, being careful not to let the liquid break through the sides.

- Support the outer walls of the mound with one hand while pushing flour from the edge of the well into the egg mixture with the other.

- Continue to incorporate ingredients until a soft dough forms.

Kneading Dough

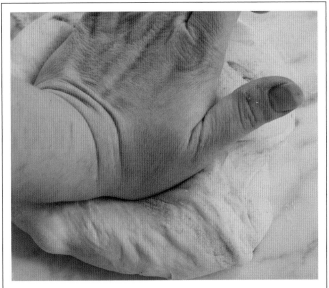

- On a floured surface, knead the dough with the heel of your hand, adding more flour if the dough is sticky.

- Knead for 5 to 10 minutes, until the dough is silky smooth and elastic throughout.

- Form the dough into a ball and place it in a lightly oiled bowl; cover with a towel or plastic wrap. Let the dough rest for 30 minutes to 2 hours. The more it rests, the easier it will be to roll out.

109

FRESH PASTA

SPINACH PASTA
The secrets of making fresh pasta—in color

Italians believe that flavor in food is more important than appearance. A different-colored food would only be of interest if the taste is enhanced as well. When it comes to pasta, adding spinach or tomato is the preferred way to do this.

Adding spinach to pasta dough gives it a vibrant green color. The dough will be harder to work because of the added moisture from the spinach; you'll need more flour per egg to achieve dough that can be rolled. Green pasta can be made with either fresh or frozen spinach that's cooked, finely chopped, squeezed of all its water, and added to the eggs before the flour is mixed in.

To make red pasta, add double-concentrated tomato paste, following the same procedure for spinach pasta.

Yield: serves 4

Ingredients:

3 large eggs

2¼ cups unbleached all-purpose flour

½ cup semolina flour

⅛ teaspoon salt

2 tablespoons chopped cooked spinach, squeezed dry

Pasta con Spinaci

- Prepare the pasta dough following directions for Classic Egg Pasta on page 108.

- Add the spinach to the well with the eggs, and beat with a fork.

- Form the dough into a ball, and place it in a lightly oiled bowl. Cover it and let it rest for 30 minutes to 2 hours.

- Roll out the dough to the desired thickness, cut it into your desired shape, and cook immediately.

Kneading Pasta: Pasta dough has to be kneaded. The kneading helps develop the gluten—the protein that makes the pasta hold together when it is cooked. To knead, place the ball on a lightly floured surface. Sprinkle the dough with flour and push it down and away with the heel of your hand. Give the dough a quarter turn and repeat until the dough is silky and elastic.

Red Pasta: Prepare the recipe as directed, but omit the spinach. Finely chop ¼ cup roasted red bell peppers (from a jar), then mash with 2 teaspoons tomato paste. Combine with the eggs and add to the flour mixture; form a dough ball, knead, and shape as desired. This dough should rest for 1 to 2 hours before rolling out and cutting.

Preparing the Spinach

Rolling Out Dough

- If the spinach is frozen, thaw it in a sieve over a bowl.

- If the spinach is fresh, remove the tough stems and wash it well. Cook the spinach leaves in a covered pot over medium heat with no additional water just until the leaves are wilted. Drain in a colander.

- Frozen or fresh, squeeze out as much water as possible.

- If you don't have a pasta machine, you can roll out the dough by hand.

- A wide wooden work surface is essential. With a wooden rolling pin, roll out the dough into a 14- by 16-inch rectangle that is about ¹⁄₁₆ inch thick.

- Starting from the center, roll outward toward the edges, giving the dough a quarter turn each time your roll it to ensure an even thickness.

FRESH PASTA

EGGLESS PASTA

If you need to avoid cholesterol, this recipe for fresh pasta offers a delicious alternative

Pasta around the world is made mostly without eggs. The addition of eggs to fresh pasta dough is strictly an Italian invention.

Basically the eggs in this recipe are replaced by oil. Incorporating more oil than usual in pasta all'uovo (egg pasta) will compensate for the eggs. This helps pasta retain its al dente bite and shape after cooking, which is what makes Italian pasta unique, wonderful, and distinctive.

Italian dry pasta is also made this way; here you simply eliminate the drying step and cook the pasta immediately. Cook fresh pasta in plenty of water (4 quarts), with salt to taste (about 1 teaspoon), until it pops to the surface (about 3 minutes). *Yield: serves 4*

Ingredients:

3 cups all-purpose flour

5 tablespoons olive oil

3/4 cup water

Eggless Pasta

- Sift the flour into a mound on a flat, smooth work surface. With your fingers, make a well in the middle.

- Pour the oil into the well. Beat the oil with a fork, gradually combining it with the surrounding flour.

- Add the water and continue blending. Continue until all of the flour and liquids have been incorporated into a ball of dough. Knead and shape the dough.

Pasta from an Electric Mixer: Pasta can be quickly made in an electric mixer instead of by hand. Combine the flour and salt, if using, in a large bowl and add the liquid ingredients. Mix on medium speed until the dough starts to form a ball and pulls away from the sides of the bowl. The dough should be silky and moist. Knead, let rest, and shape as directed.

ZOOM

Drying Pasta: While homemade pasta can be cooked immediately, you can also dry it for later use. There are pasta-drying racks, but you can use anything that is clean and will hold the pasta off the counter. A clothes drying rack is ideal. Lay the strands of fresh pasta over the rack and let them dry in a warm place for several hours until they're brittle. Store in an airtight container.

Cooking Fresh Pasta

- Fresh pasta cooks much faster than dried pasta. Because it's fresh, pasta cut like vermicelli, spaghetti, and fettuccine will cook in less than 3 minutes. Fresh lasagna noodles and stuffed pasta will take just a few minutes longer.

- You can check for doneness by tasting a strand or two of the cooked pasta. When it's done, drain the pasta by pouring it carefully into a colander in the sink.

Pasta at Rest

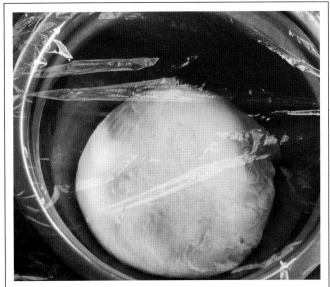

- Knead the dough until a smooth ball is formed. Then let the dough rest. This is a very important step in the pasta-making process.

- The dough should rest on a floured surface covered with a bowl, a damp kitchen towel, or plastic wrap.

- Resting the dough allows the gluten in the dough to relax, which will make it easier to roll out.

TAGLIATELLE WITH SAUCE

Italy is well known for its mouthwatering sauces like this one below

Italy, being a land of traditions, has little interest in creating new sauce recipes. Instead, cooks apply their individual touch to already existing sauces and pestos. All of them swear that the one they make is the best, and it probably is. This recipe comes from Bologna.

When I was a child, along with my siblings, I could hardly wait for my mother to bring to the table a platter full of freshly made tagliatelle, topped with Bolognese sauce. The aroma of it would engulf the whole house and force all of us to keep asking our mother every five minutes "It is ready yet?" This drove my mother crazy, but made her smile proudly in the affirmation that her sauce was still the best.

Yield: serves 4–6

Ingredients:

3 tablespoons extra-virgin olive oil

5 tablespoons butter, divided

2 tablespoons finely chopped onion

2 tablespoons finely diced carrot

2 tablespoons finely diced celery

³/₄ pound coarsely ground lean beef

Salt, to taste

1 cup dry white wine

¹/₂ cup whole milk

¹/₂ teaspoon freshly ground nutmeg

2 cups canned whole peeled tomatoes, with juice, coarsely chopped

Egg pasta (recipe on page 108)

¹/₂ cup freshly grated Parmigiano Reggiano cheese

Tagliatelle with Sauce

- In a deep saucepan, over medium-high heat, combine oil and 3 tablespoons of butter. Sauté the onion, carrot, and celery until soft. Add ground beef and salt. Cook until meat is browned.

- Add wine and let it completely evaporate. Stir in milk, nutmeg and tomatoes. Simmer, uncovered, for 3 hours, stirring occasionally,

- In a large pot, bring salted water to a boil. Add tagliatelle, and cook for 3 minutes. Drain and toss with hot sauce, remaining butter, and freshly grated cheese.

Mushroom Ragu: Prepare the recipe as directed, except increase the onion to ¼ cup finely chopped. Omit the beef and substitute 8 ounces cremini mushrooms, sliced, and 4 ounces shiitake mushrooms, sliced. Substitute dry red wine for the white wine, and use ½ cup light cream in pace of the whole milk. Finish the recipe by cooking the pasta and adding cheese and salt.

Sausage Ragu: Prepare the recipe as directed, but increase the onion, carrot, and celery to ¼ cup each. Omit the beef; substitute 1 pound mild or hot Italian sausage. After the sausage is browned, drain off excess fat, then proceed with the recipe, using red wine in place of white. Substitute grated Pecorino Romano cheese for Parmigiano.

Sautéing Vegetables

- The basis of this sauce is a trio of aromatic vegetables that should be finely diced.

- First, sauté the onions until they turn a light golden color.

- Next sauté the carrots and celery until they begin to change color and soften.

Draining Pasta

- The best way to cook pasta is in a large-capacity pasta pot with a colander insert that allows you to easily lift the pasta out of the boiling water to drain.

- Or you can use a large pot without an insert. To drain, place a colander in the sink. Pour the pasta from the pot into the colander.

- With delicate filled pasta, use a pasta scoop or slotted spoon to gently remove the pieces from the water.

FRESH PASTA

GNOCCHI ROMAN-STYLE
Imagine eating a dish first prepared by ancient Romans

A long time ago when gnocchi were first invented by the ancient Romans, they were made with only flour and water. It wasn't until much later, at the beginning of the last century, that potatoes were introduced to Italians by the Austrians. Austrians knew how to incorporate this starchy vegetable into pasta dough.

Italian chefs immediately recognized the potential of this new vegetable and adopted the Austrian technique, which brought gnocchi making to another level. But even with this new recipe, the original Roman gnocchi recipe was far from being forgotten.

This is the original Roman recipe for gnocchi; it does not contain potatoes. It is very easy to make, and the taste is like no other.

Yield: serves 10

Ingredients

1¹/₄ cups milk

10 tablespoons (1¹/₄ sticks) butter, divided

¹/₂ teaspoon salt

¹/₄ teaspoon nutmeg

9 ounces semolina

5 ounces grated Parmigiano Reggiano cheese, divided

2 egg yolks

Gnocchi Roman-Style

- Preheat the oven to 450°F. Combine the milk, ¼ cup (½ stick) of the butter, salt, and nutmeg in a saucepan. Bring to a boil.

- Sprinkle the semolina into the hot milk, and stir over low heat for 15 minutes. Add 2 ounces of grated cheese and the egg yolks.

Blend thoroughly.

- Spread the mixture into a 1-inch-deep buttered sheet pan. Cool. Cut into slices.

- Sprinkle the remainder of the grated cheese and butter over the gnocchi. Bake for 10 to 15 minutes, until a golden yellow crust forms.

Potato Gnocchi: Bake 2 large russet potatoes at 400°F for 50 minutes. Cut them open and let them cool for 30 minutes, then remove the flesh from the skin. Push the flesh through a potato ricer and add 1 beaten egg, 1¼ cups semolina flour, ½ teaspoon salt, and ⅛ teaspoon pepper; mix well. Form into a rope, then cut into 1-inch pieces. Cook in boiling water until they float.

ZOOM

Semolina is flour made from durum wheat. It is yellow because of the carotenoid pigments in the grain, a form of vitamin A. It's coarser than the all-purpose flour you're used to seeing. True semolina flour is necessary to reproduce the color and flavor of Roman gnocchi. Semolina is high in protein and vitamins folate, thiamine, and niacin.

Adding the Semolina

- Semolina is ground durum wheat used to make gnocchi, pasta, bread, and other foods. Durum flour is the hardest and contains the most protein of all wheat flours.

- Semolina has a deep golden yellow color, and it's used in the commercial production of dried pasta.

- Semolina, added to water, produces a dough that is strong enough to pass through an extruder to make hundreds of different pasta cuts.

Cutting Slices

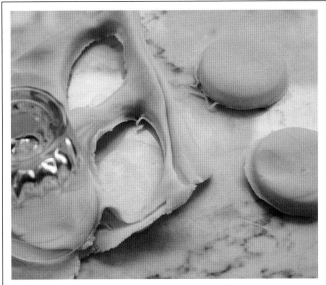

- Once the semolina mixture on the sheet pan is cool, you can cut it into slices.

- Using a cookie cutter or an empty glass, cut the cooked semolina into round slices 1¾ to 2 inches in diameter.

- Layer these round slices in a buttered baking dish so that the edges of each slice overlap.

FRESH PASTA

STUFFED TORTELLONI

This recipe is a mouthwatering specialty using flavorful prosciutto and a rich blend of cheeses

Tortelloni can be filled with myriad mouthwatering stuffings. With only a few exceptions, all the other stuffed pasta shapes are easy to make and require no special skills. The biggest problem in making stuffed pasta will be trying to work with sheets of pasta that are too dry. To help avoid this, always keep dough tightly wrapped in plastic until you are ready to use it.

You could also add about 2 teaspoons of milk to a 2-egg batch of dough when you mix the eggs.

This delectable recipe calls for prosciutto, an Italian specialty, most often imported from the Italian city of Parma. Prosciutto is a ham cured without smoke and sliced paper-thin.

Yield: serves 6

Ingredients:

Fresh tortelloni (recipe on page 108)

Filling:

4 ounces prosciutto

1 cup ricotta

$\frac{1}{2}$ pound fresh mozzarella, shredded

3 tablespoons grated Parmigiano Reggiano cheese

1 egg

1 tablespoon fresh or 1 teaspoon dried chopped parsley

Salt and pepper, to taste

Stuffed Tortelloni

- Cut the prosciutto into pieces about ⅛-inch square. Combine all the ingredients in a bowl and mix well.

- For the tortelloni: Follow the recipe for making fresh pasta on page 108.

- Stuff the pasta with the filling mixture.

- Fresh pasta needs to cook for only 3 minutes from the time it is dropped into boiling water. Drain carefully to avoid breakage and the fillings leaking out.

Pesto Tortelloni: Prepare the recipe as directed, but with a different filling: In a medium bowl, combine ⅓ cup basil pesto with ½ cup ricotta, ⅓ cup minced sun-dried tomatoes in oil, ¼ cup grated Parmigiano Reggiano cheese, 1 egg, 1 cup shredded mozzarella, and 1 cup shredded Fontina cheese. Stuff the pasta and proceed as directed.

Mushroom Tortelloni: Prepare recipe, but with a different filling: Cook ¼ cup minced onion, 2 minced garlic cloves, and 2 cups finely chopped cremini mushrooms in 2 tablespoons olive oil until mushrooms are tender and liquid has evaporated. Let cool, then mix with 1 egg, ⅓ cup ricotta, and ½ cup grated Parmesan. Season with salt, pepper, and 1 teaspoon dried oregano. Fill the pasta as directed.

Preparing the Stuffing and Shaping Tortelloni

Stuffing Tortelloni

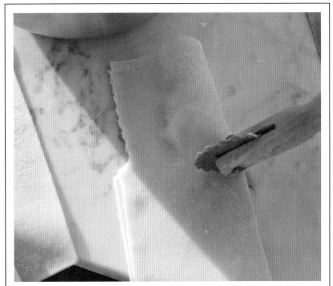

- Tortelloni are a large version of tortelli, which are in turn similar to ravioli.

- Grate the Parmigiano Reggiano, shred the fresh mozzarella and mix with ricotta, egg, parsley, salt, and pepper.

- Take a strip of pasta sheet 4 inches wide and place stuffing on it at 2-inch intervals. You need the equivalent of a rounded teaspoon of stuffing.

- On the lower half of a long strip of pasta 4 inches wide, place a rounded teaspoon of stuffing at 2-inch intervals.

- Moisten the edges of the pasta, and fold the top of the pasta strip over the bottom half.

- Using a flute cutter, cut between the mounds of stuffing at 2-inch intervals. Trim the bottom edge for a neat finish.

- Pinch the edges together to seal tightly.

FRESH PASTA

RISOTTO ALLA MILANESE

Saffron gives Risotto alla Milanese its distinctive flavor

The spice saffron, which is still relatively expensive, is essential to risotto alla Milanese. Saffron is the ingredient that gives this dish its distinctive golden color.

Before using this spice, the threads should be crushed in a mortar and pestle (which can be found in any kitchen specialty shop) and left to infuse in a little warm water to release the flavor. The risotto should be creamy and moist but not wet.

There is a wonderful story about how this dish got its name. Legend has it that the dish dates back to 1574, when a stained-glass worker in Milan, who was known for the yellow color of his glass, colored the rice at the wedding of his boss's daughter with the same saffron he used to tint his stained glass.
Yield: serves 4

Ingredients:

1 onion

¹/₄ cup butter, divided

1¹/₂ cups arborio rice

¹/₂ cup dry white wine

1 quart hot chicken, beef, or vegetable stock

¹/₈–¹/₄ teaspoon crumbled saffron threads (can be found in any specialty food shop)

2 ounces Parmigiano Reggiano cheese, freshly grated

Salt and freshly ground pepper

Risotto alla Milanese

- Peel and finely chop the onion, melt 2 tablespoons of the butter in a saucepan, and sauté the onion until translucent.

- Stir in the rice and wine. Add the hot stock to the rice one ladleful at a time until absorbed, stirring constantly (see technique).

- After the risotto starts to get creamy, dissolve the saffron in the last of the stock.

- Stir the rest of the butter into the rice. Add the freshly, grated cheese, and season with salt and pepper.

120

···· RECIPE VARIATION ····

Arancini di Riso: Prepare the recipe as directed, except when the risotto is done, stir in 2 eggs and another ½ cup Parmigiano Reggiano cheese. Spread in a shallow pan and place in the refrigerator; cool completely. Form into balls using ¼ cup for each; press one 1-inch cube of mozzarella in the center. Roll in ½ cup flour, 2 beaten eggs, and 1 cup dried bread crumbs. Fry in 1 cup olive oil until crisp.

Herbed Risotto: Prepare the recipe as directed, but omit the saffron threads. Add 3 minced garlic cloves along with the onion. When you add the rice to the pan, add ½ teaspoon each dried basil and dried thyme. Cook the risotto as directed. When the rice is cooked, stir in 2 tablespoons each chopped fresh basil, fresh parsley, fresh thyme, and softened butter. Cover; let stand for 5 minutes and serve.

Pouring in Rice and Wine

- Pour the rice into the pan and stir it into the buttery onions over very low heat, until it turns whitish and translucent. Don't let it turn brown. Pour in the wine and a ladle of hot stock, and stir well.

- With the pan uncovered, keep stirring the rice while cooking. The liquid is not only absorbed by the rice, but also evaporates and must be replaced with another ladleful of stock as it's absorbed.

- You will notice that the mixture suddenly turns creamy.

Dissolving the Saffron

- After the risotto starts to get creamy, add the saffron to the last of the stock. Stir and allow to dissolve.

- Add the last of the stock to the pan; stir gently. The rice will be drenched in a rich deep-yellow color.

- Take a bite to taste whether those soft-looking grains of rice still have a slightly firm center, indicating a perfectly cooked risotto.

RISOTTO WITH FRUIT

Incorporating fruit in cooking is one of the most elegant and creative ways of adopting Italian cuisine

Italian rice is regularly checked by the National Rice Institute to make sure that the quality and the nutritional content of the various types are constant.

Rice is divided into four categories: *riso comune* (household rice), used for desserts and soups (when cooked it gets soft); *riso superfino* (superfine rice), which makes a great risotto; *riso*

semifino (with round grains), used for minestrone or as a side dish; and *riso fino* (medium grain size), good for risotto, side dishes, salads, and soups.

In the Alto Adige region of Italy, risotto is combined with fruit. It looks very elegant and tastes incredible. It is a beautiful example of high-style Italian cuisine. *Yield: serves 6*

Ingredients:

4¹/₂–5 cups homemade chicken broth (store-bought is fine; low-sodium if possible)

6 tablespoons (³/₄ stick) butter

¹/₂ cup finely minced onion

2 cups arborio rice (available in any supermarket)

1 cup dry white wine, such as Frascati

1 cup fresh blueberries

Risotto with Fruit

- In a saucepan, bring the chicken broth to a simmer. Keep warm over low heat.

- In a large saucepan, melt the butter over medium heat. Add the onion and sauté until very soft. Add the rice, wine, and chicken broth. Continue to simmer, stirring constantly.

- The rice should be al dente, not mushy. Add, if necessary, up to ½ cup more broth. Reduce the heat to low and add the fruit. Stir to lightly mash the fruit. Cook for 3 to 4 minutes, or until the fruit is softened. Serve at once.

•••• RECIPE VARIATIONS ••••

Sparkling Risotto with Fruit: Prepare recipe as directed, except substitute sparkling Asti Spumanti for the dry white wine. You can also use any sparkling dry white wine, including champagne. When the rice is perfectly cooked, stir in 1 tablespoon butter, 1 tablespoon minced fresh thyme leaves, and ½ cup more fresh blueberries. Be sure the berries are rinsed and dried before adding to the risotto.

Mixed Berry Risotto: Prepare the recipe as directed, but substitute ½ cup each blueberries, raspberries, and strawberries for the fresh blueberries. Stir in another ½ cup of fresh berries just before serving. Garnish the risotto with sprigs of fresh thyme or fresh mint. Do not substitute frozen berries for the fresh, as they will add too much water to the recipe.

Berry Basics

- To enjoy fresh blueberries throughout the year, place them unwashed in a single layer on a baking sheet, and freeze them. Remove the pan from the freezer, place the berries in plastic bags, and return them to the freezer for up to 6 months.

- Fresh, dried, or frozen berries should not be washed until you are about to serve them or use them in a recipe.

- Risotto can also be paired with fresh strawberries, which should be rinsed, trimmed, and quartered.

Cooking in Stages

- Add the rice; cook for 1 to 2 minutes, stirring to coat each grain with the butter and onion mixture. Reduce the heat to medium-low; add ½ cup wine.

- Cook, stirring constantly, until the wine is absorbed. Add ½ cup chicken broth; cook, continuing to stir, until the rice has absorbed the liquid.

- Add the remaining ½ cup wine; then add 4 cups of broth ½ a cup at a time, continuing to stir and allowing the rice to absorb each addition.

RISOTTO WITH ASPARAGUS

Embrace spring and serve your family a platter of this colorful asparagus dish

The ways to flavor risotto are endless, and depending on what is in season, the presentation can change dramatically. This dish requires arborio rice, which is a member of the superfine rice family. It takes 18 minutes to cook and has lots of starch to preserve the moistness and juiciness of the grains throughout the cooking process and after.

Three types of asparagus are grown in Italy: green, grown mainly in Piedmont; a purple variety called *asparago Napolitano* because it is grown in Campania; and white, grown only in the Veneto region. You could serve this dish with fish, chicken, or beef, or by itself as a light summer dinner. Everybody will be happy with this choice. *Yield: serves 3*

Ingredients:

4 cups chicken broth (homemade or low-salt canned)

1 pound asparagus, sliced on diagonal (save tough ends for stock)

2 cups sliced shiitake mushrooms (¹/₄ inch thick)

1 cup finely chopped onions

¹/₄ cup extra virgin olive oil

Salt and ground black pepper

1 tablespoon minced garlic

1 cup arborio rice

¹/₂ cup dry white wine (optional)

1¹/₂ teaspoons finely chopped fresh thyme

1 tablespoon unsalted butter

¹/₄ cup coarsely grated Fontina cheese

³/₄ cup freshly grated Parmigiano Reggiano cheese, divided

1¹/₂ tablespoons finely chopped fresh Italian parsley

1¹/₂ teaspoons freshly grated lemon zest

Risotto with Asparagus

- Bring the broth to a boil. Add the tough asparagus stems; simmer until tender, 7 minutes. Discard stems.

- Brown mushrooms and onions in olive oil; cook until soft, 2 minutes. Season with salt and pepper. Add the garlic and rice; stir for 2 minutes.

- Add the wine, thyme, mushrooms, and asparagus. Cook until rice is al dente and asparagus is bright green and tender, 4 minutes.

- Remove from heat; stir in butter, Fontina, ½ cup of Parmigiano, parsley, and lemon zest. Sprinkle with remaining cheese.

• • • • RECIPE VARIATION • • • •

Risotto with Peas: Prepare recipe except substitute 1 pound fresh or frozen small peas for asparagus. Do not use asparagus in chicken broth. Omit the shiitake mushrooms; substitute cremini or portobello mushrooms, thinly sliced. Add peas when cooked mushrooms are added. Increase the Parmigiano Reggiano cheese to 1 cup. Garnish with fresh thyme sprigs.

ZOOM

About Risotto: Risotto is made with arborio rice, a short-grain rice with lots of highly branched starch molecules. The slow cooking, stirring action, and gradual addition of liquids coaxes more starch out of the rice and into the liquid. This makes the risotto creamy and thick without flour or other thickeners.

Preparing Vegetables

- Rinse the asparagus and gently wipe the mushrooms before use.

- Snap off the hard ends from the asparagus, and peel any tough skin from the stalks.

- Heat the olive oil in a heavy medium saucepan over medium-high heat until hot.

- Brown the mushrooms and onions for about 1 minute. Season with salt and pepper; sauté until tender, about 5 minutes. Remove to a plate.

Adding Wine and Stock

- Add wine to the rice, and cook until the pan is nearly dry. Adjust the heat to a low simmer.

- Add ½ cup of stock; stir and cook until the pan is almost dry again.

- Season lightly with salt and pepper, and add another ½ cup of stock.

- Continue to stir and cook, adding stock as necessary until the rice is almost done, about 15 minutes.

RISOTTO WITH MEAT SAUCE

Less expensive, tougher cuts of meat are better suited for this long-cooking ragu

Emilia-Romagna is home to this tasty dish, which uses a meat ragu and the soaking liquid from porcini mushrooms instead of the traditional broth and wine.

Except for a few species, mushrooms do not need washing; the best way to clean them is to wipe them with a damp cloth to remove any dirt. Remove the stem to check for insects. Never peel mushrooms; the skin contains lots of nutrients and flavor. To prevent mushrooms from discoloring, coat them with lemon juice after cutting.

To reconstitute dried mushrooms, soak them in warm water for 30 minutes, drain, and save the liquid for later use.
Yield: serves 8

Ingredients:

1 cup dried porcini mushrooms (about 1 ounce)

6 tablespoons (³/₄ stick) butter

2 cups arborio rice

2 tablespoons heavy cream

1 cup freshly grated Parmigiano Reggiano cheese

Ragu:

¹/₄ cup olive oil

1 white onion, thinly sliced

¹/₂ pound sweet Italian sausage, casings removed

2 cups chopped fresh or canned plum tomatoes (about 4 medium)

¹/₂ cup water

Salt, to taste

Risotto with Meat Sauce

- Prep the mushrooms. Make the ragu.

- Melt butter over medium heat. Add rice; cook for 1 to 2 minutes, stirring. When rice begins to crackle, reduce heat to medium-low and add ¼ cup of reserved porcini liquid. Cook, stirring, until absorbed. Add ¼ cup of ragu and cook, stirring, until absorbed. Add remaining porcini liquid and sauce to rice alternately, ¼ cup at a time, letting the rice absorb all liquid before adding more.

- Stir in cream. Remove from heat; stir in cheese.

・・・・ RECIPE VARIATIONS ・・・・

Beef Ragu Risotto: Prepare recipe but substitute the following sauce: Cook 1 chopped yellow onion with 3 minced garlic cloves in ¼ cup olive oil. Add 1 pound chuck steak, cut into 1-inch pieces; cook until browned. Add 4 chopped tomatoes, 1 cup water, salt and pepper to taste, and 1 teaspoon dried oregano. Simmer, covered, for one hour until beef is tender. Shred beef and complete recipe.

Chicken Risotto: Prepare recipe but omit Italian sausage and tomatoes from the ragu. Cut 6 boneless, skinless chicken thighs into 1-inch pieces. When the onion is cooked, add chicken; cook, stirring frequently, until browned, about 7 minutes. Add 1 cup chicken broth; simmer for 10 minutes. Use this in place of the ragu when making the risotto.

Prepping Porcini Mushrooms

- Put the porcini mushrooms and 4 cups of cold water in a large bowl. Set aside to soak until soft, about 30 minutes.

- Drain the mushrooms in a colander set over a bowl.

- Dice the mushrooms; set aside. Strain the porcini liquid several times to remove any sand. Pour it into a saucepan, and bring it to barely a boil. Keep warm over very low heat.

Making the Ragu

- In a large skillet, heat the oil, add the onion, and sauté until golden brown and almost caramelized.

- Add the sausages, breaking apart the meat and browning it. Stir in the tomatoes, ½ cup water, and salt, mixing well.

- Let simmer until thickened, about 15 minutes. Transfer to a food processor and blend until smooth.

- Put the ragu in a bowl; set aside.

RISOTTO FRITTATA

For a dramatic color contrast, select the excellent and beautiful color of saffron

Rice and rice dishes have an important place in Italian cuisine. Milanese chefs prefer to use arborio rice for this creation. Half omelet, half risotto, this dish makes a delightful and satisfying appetizer. If possible, cook each frittata separately and preferably in a small cast-iron pan, so that the eggs can cook quickly underneath but stay moist on top.

This dish can also be cooked in a large pan and served in wedges. Don't be impatient while cooking the rice. Adding the stock gradually ensures a wonderfully creamy consistency. Milanese risotto obtains its color from saffron, which is an expensive spice known mostly for giving a warm yellow color to this and other dishes. *Yield: serves 4*

KNACK ITALIAN COOKING

Ingredients:

2-3 tablespoons olive oil, divided

1 small onion, finely chopped

1 garlic clove, crushed

1 large red bell pepper, seeded and cut into thin strips

³/₄ cup arborio rice

1²/₃-2 cups simmering vegetable stock

2-3 tablespoons butter

2¹/₂ cups finely sliced button mushrooms

¹/₄ cup freshly grated Parmesan cheese

6-8 eggs, beaten

Salt and ground black pepper

Risotto Frittata

- Heat 1 tablespoon of oil in a large frying pan. Fry onions and garlic over low heat for 2 to 3 minutes, until onions are soft but not brown. Add pepper; cook, stirring, for 4 to 5 minutes, until soft.

- Add rice. Add stock in stages, allowing rice to absorb each addition.

- Continue cooking until rice is al dente.

- In a separate pan, heat remaining oil and butter. Fry mushrooms until golden.

- Remove rice from heat; stir in mushrooms, Parmesan, and beaten eggs. Season.

• • • • RECIPE VARIATION • • • •

Bread Crumb Frittata: Make frittata omitting risotto mixture. Cook 1 chopped onion and 2 garlic cloves in 2 tablespoons olive oil until tender. Add 1 cup buttered whole-grain bread crumbs and sauté until golden. Beat 8 eggs with 2 tablespoons water, salt, and pepper and add to skillet. Cook gently until frittata is set; top with ⅓ cup shredded Parmesan cheese. Let stand 3 minutes.

ZOOM

Arborio rice is a special type of rice always used when making risotto. It's a short-grain rice full of amylopectin, a starch molecule with lots of branches. This type of starch holds lots of liquid and makes the rice moist and sticky when it's cooked, creating the proper risotto consistency. Do not substitute long- or medium-grain rice for arborio.

Rice Done Right

- When you add the rice to the frying pan, it's important that you stir it gently until the grains are evenly coated with oil. Continue stirring and cooking for 2 to 3 minutes.

- Add the hot stock to the rice in stages, approximately ½ cup at a time.

- Stir constantly until the liquid is absorbed by the rice before adding another ½ cup of stock.

Beating and Adding Eggs

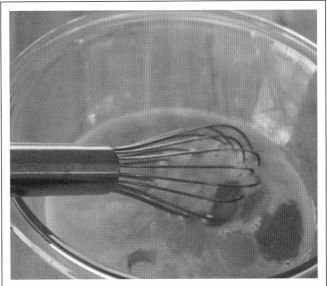

- In a large bowl, beat the eggs together with 8 teaspoons cold water; season well with salt and pepper.

- In the large frying pan, spread the hot risotto mixture out evenly. Immediately add the beaten eggs.

- Cook over medium-high heat for 1 to 2 minutes, or until the eggs are cooked, then transfer to a warmed plate and serve.

129

FOUR-CHEESE RISOTTO

This is a rich dish for special occasions; serve it with a light, sparkling white wine

Most people outside Italy use hard cheeses only for cooking, not realizing how wonderful a freshly cut chunk of Parmigiano Reggiano or Pecorino Toscano is with San Daniele ham, fresh figs, and a glass of medium-bodied red wine.

Italians call these cheeses *formaggi di tavola*, which loosely means that hard cheeses are always kept on the table so people can snack on them all day. Cheeses in Italy are seldom found outside the region in which they are made.

This dish is yet another example of Italian cuisine at its best. The flavors of the four cheeses combined with the creaminess of the arborio rice make this dish unforgettable.
Yield: serves 6

Ingredients:

3 tablespoons butter

1 small onion, finely chopped

5 cups chicken stock (low-sodium preferred)

1³/₄ cups arborio rice

1 cup dry white wine

¹/₂ cup grated Gruyère cheese

¹/₂ cup diced Taleggio cheese (available in cheese shops and Italian markets)

¹/₂ cup diced Gorgonzola cheese

²/₃ cup freshly grated Parmigiano Reggiano cheese, divided

Salt and ground black pepper, to taste

Italian parsley, as needed to garnish

Four-Cheese Risotto

- Melt butter in a large saucepan; fry the onion over low heat for 4 to 5 minutes, stirring frequently, until it's softened and light browned. Pour stock into a separate pan and bring to a simmer.

- Add rice, wine, and stock to the saucepan.

- Gradually add remaining stock, letting rice absorb liquid before adding more. After 25 minutes, rice will be al dente and risotto will have a creamy consistency.

- Turn off heat; add cheeses. Pass the remaining Parmigiano separately. Season to taste. Garnish with parsley.

···· RECIPE VARIATION ····

Pink Risotto with Three Cheeses: Prepare the recipe as directed, except use 1 cup dry red wine in place of the dry white wine. You can use beef stock in place of half of the chicken stock for a deeper, richer flavor. Use Fontina, Gruyère, and Parmigiano-Reggiano cheeses to finish the dish, and stir in 1 tablespoon butter along with the cheeses.

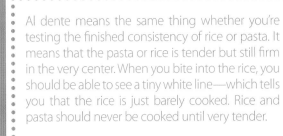

ZOOM

Al dente means the same thing whether you're testing the finished consistency of rice or pasta. It means that the pasta or rice is tender but still firm in the very center. When you bite into the rice, you should be able to see a tiny white line—which tells you that the rice is just barely cooked. Rice and pasta should never be cooked until very tender.

Frying the Onion and Adding the Rice

- Add the rice to the onion mixture; stir until the grains of rice start to swell and burst, then add the wine.

- Stir until it stops sizzling and most of the wine has been absorbed by the rice.

- Pour in a little of the stock. Add salt and pepper to taste.

- Stir the rice constantly over low heat until all the stock has been absorbed.

Adding the Cheeses

- Once the risotto has a creamy texture, turn off the heat and add the Gruyère, Taleggio, Gorgonzola, and 2 tablespoons of the Parmigiano Reggiano.

- Stir gently until cheeses have melted. Taste for seasoning.

- Spoon into a serving bowl and garnish with parsley.

VEAL IN LEMON SAUCE

Good veal is so tender that it almost melts in your mouth

Some of the most flavorful beef in Italy comes from Tuscany because of the natural grazing available to the animals. Meat from this region is low in fat without being dry and has a certain spiciness to it. These animals, which can grow to more than 1,000 pounds, provide the T-bone steaks used in *bistecca alla Fiorentina*.

Veal is very popular in Italy, especially in the northern regions. Calves are milk-fed and then butchered when only a few months old. This accounts for veal's tenderness. Because veal is almost flavorless, the success of a veal dish depends on the sauce, seasoning, and stuffing used.

Yield: serves 4

Ingredients:

2 tablespoons butter

1 pound veal cutlets, cut into 1/2-inch-wide strips

Salt and ground black pepper, to taste

4 large eggs, beaten

Juice of 2 lemons

1/4 cup finely chopped fresh parsley

Veal in Lemon Sauce

- In a large skillet, melt the butter over medium-high heat. Season the veal strips with salt and pepper; fry until browned. Remove the veal strips and cover to keep warm.

- In a saucepan, combine the eggs and lemon. Cook, whisking constantly, for 8 minutes, or until the mixture is thick enough to coat the back of a spoon.

- Lower the heat, add the veal strips and cook, stirring, for about 2 minutes or until heated through. Transfer the meat and sauce to serving platter, and sprinkle with parsley.

Veal with Capers: Prepare the recipe as directed, but sauté 2 garlic cloves in the butter before adding the veal. Remove the garlic and discard, then cook the veal. When the egg and lemon sauce are cooked, stir in 2 tablespoons capers with the veal. Sprinkle the finished dish with ¼ cup finely chopped fresh basil and ½ teaspoon grated lemon rind.

Veal in Orange Sauce: Prepare recipe except omit lemon juice. After veal has been browned and removed, add 2 minced shallots to drippings in pan; sauté until tender. Beat eggs with ½ cup freshly squeezed orange juice and add to pan; cook as directed. Return veal to pan and stir in parsley along with 1 teaspoon grated orange zest and 1 tablespoon fresh thyme leaves.

Using a Double Boiler

- The lemon sauce in this recipe can be made easily in a double boiler.

- Combine the eggs and lemon juice in the top of a large double boiler that is set over simmering water.

- Whisk constantly, for 8 minutes, or until the mixture is thick enough to coat the back of a spoon.

Preparing Veal

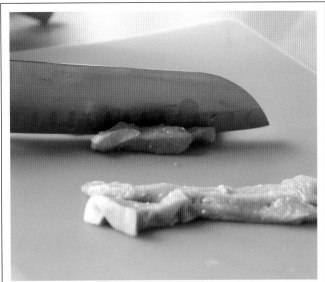

- Veal is a tender meat, but it can be made even more tender if pounded with a meat mallet.

- Place the veal cutlets on a sheet of plastic wrap or

waxed paper. Cover with another sheet, and pound the entire cutlet.

- For this recipe, cut the veal cutlets into strips that are ½ inch wide.

VEAL MARSALA

This easy-to-prepare dish is one of the most popular and recognizable anywhere

This dish literally takes minutes to prepare. Best of all, your family and friends will assume you spent a lot a time in the kitchen to impress them.

When sautéing small pieces of meat, do not crowd the pan, and do not flip or toss the food more than a few times. This will cause the temperature of the oil to drop, and the food will simmer in its own juices instead of sautéing.

Use a mixture of olive oil and butter when sautéing; using only butter will burn. Dredging the meat in flour will make it cook and brown more evenly, and it prevents sticking. Do not flour the meat too far in advance, however, or it will become pasty. *Yield: serves 6*

KNACK ITALIAN COOKING

Ingredients:

2 pounds veal cutlets, $^{1}/_{8}$ inch thick

$^{1}/_{2}$ cup flour, seasoned with salt and white pepper

6–8 tablespoons ($^{3}/_{4}$–1 stick) butter, divided

$^{2}/_{3}$ cup Marsala wine, dry or sweet

$^{1}/_{2}$ cup fresh lemon juice

Lemon wedges, for garnish

Parsley sprigs, for garnish

Veal Marsala

- Dredge the cutlets in flour.

- In a large frying pan, heat 4 tablespoons of the butter; add some cutlets. Cook for 1 minute on each side. Remove to a warm platter. Repeat, adding butter to the pan as needed.

- Add the wine and lemon juice to the pan; simmer over medium heat, scraping the bottom of the pan with a wooden spoon to release the brown bits. Return all the veal to the pan to heat through. Transfer the meat to a serving platter, pour the pan juices over it, and garnish with lemon wedges and parsley sprigs.

Veal Scaloppine with Lemon: Prepare the recipe as directed, except substitute 6 tablespoons lemon juice and ¼ cup limoncello (lemon liqueur) for the Marsala wine. Cook as directed. After plating, top each piece of veal with a very thinly sliced piece of lemon and sprinkle with chopped Italian flat-leaf parsley.

Veal Scaloppine alla Crème: Prepare the recipe as directed, but omit the Marsala wine. Deglaze the pan with ⅓ cup low-sodium vegetable broth. Add 1 cup heavy cream and simmer the sauce over low heat for 10 to 12 minutes, until thickened. Omit the butter. Season the veal with a few drops of lemon juice and taste for seasoning; return to the sauce and heat through.

Dredging Cutlets

- Dredging meat helps it cook more consistently.

- In a bowl, mix the flour with 1½ teaspoons of salt and 1 teaspoon of pepper, and spread it on a large flat plate.

- Dredge each cutlet in the seasoned flour, shaking off the excess.

Sautéing Cutlets

- Care must be taken in cooking veal cutlets, or they can become tough and chewy.

- Cook only a few cutlets at a time. Do not crowd the cutlets in the frying pan.

- Be careful not to overcook the veal. Just 1 or 2 minutes on each side, or until the meat is no longer pink, is all that is needed.

VEAL WITH PIZZA SAUCE

If you like pizza, you will adore this recipe, as it shares a lot of the same ingredients

When cooking with meat, use only small pieces for sautéing. Smaller or thinner pieces require higher heat. The object is to cook or sear the meat in the time it takes to cook it.

Sautéing small pieces of meat requires small quantities of fat. If you toss the pieces in the pan, all sides come in contact with the heat. When pan-frying more than one batch, strain the fat between batches.

Italians are always creating new dishes or refreshing old ones. I am especially proud of this recipe with fresh tomato sauce. It is tender as a cloud and just spicy enough. This dish is a favorite for when company is over because it can be prepared in just a few minutes. *Yield: serves 4*

Veal with Pizza Sauce

KNACK ITALIAN COOKING

Ingredients:

¹/₄ cup olive oil

3 garlic cloves, finely chopped

4 cups coarsely chopped fresh plum tomatoes (canned is fine)—about 8 medium-size tomatoes

2 teaspoons salt

1¹/₂ tablespoons chopped fresh oregano or 1 tablespoon dried

¹/₄ cup chopped fresh basil

2 tablespoons butter

1 pound veal cutlets

¹/₂ cup flour, seasoned with salt and white pepper

¹/₄ cup chopped fresh parsley

- In a large skillet, heat the oil and sauté the garlic until soft. Add the tomatoes, salt, and oregano.

- Simmer over low heat for about 15 minutes, or until slightly thickened. Remove from the heat; stir in the basil, and set aside.

- Season the veal. In a large skillet, melt the butter, add the veal, and sauté until lightly brown on both sides, about 2 minutes. Add the tomato sauce and simmer for about 5 minutes. Stir in the parsley.

Steak with Pizza Sauce: Prepare the recipe as directed, but substitute 1 pound sirloin steak for the veal. Season the steak with salt and pepper and drizzle with olive oil. Sear the steak on both sides in a hot skillet, then reduce the heat and cook until tender, about 5 to 6 minutes. Let the steak rest while you prepare the sauce. Thinly slice the steak and serve sauce over it.

Veal Parmigiana: Omit the sauce. Prepare the veal as directed, seasoning with salt and pepper. Melt the butter in a pan and cook the veal as directed. Top each cutlet with ¼ cup tomato sauce, a thin slice of fresh mozzarella cheese, and 2 tablespoons of freshly grated Parmigiano Reggiano. Pass under the broiler for 2 to 3 minutes to melt the cheese. Serve immediately.

Prepping the Veal

- Pat the veal dry with a paper towel.

- With a meat mallet, pound all the veal cutlets between sheets of plastic wrap or waxed paper.

- Season the veal cutlets on both sides with salt and pepper.

- Right before cooking, dredge the veal cutlets in the seasoned flour. Shake off any excess flour.

Combining the Veal and Sauce

- With two skillets going on the stove, you can add the veal to the sauce, or you can add the sauce to the skillet containing the veal.

- With either technique, turn the veal cutlets in the sauce to heat the meat through and to coat every cutlet with the sauce.

BRACIOLA STUFFED W/VEGETABLES

This is a great way to combine beef and vegetables in an exciting dish

This particular dish is often found in Italian restaurants. Sometimes it's not on the menu, and you have to ask for it. Accommodating chefs will make it for customers who have heard about the dish by word of mouth. Usually the *cameriere* (waiter) will list the available dishes of the day at the table, and sometime the chef will ask customers what they would like to eat.

Because this dish requires a grill, it is a perfect summer food. Eating alfresco with family and friends is the most enjoyable part of the summer. The laughter of children, lively conversation, and, of course, the smell of good food cooking on the grill are the things we remember most. This dish reminds me of those times. *Yield: serves 4*

Ingredients:

¹/₄ cup low-sodium soy sauce

2 tablespoons packed light brown sugar

1 pound beef tenderloin

4 green onions, green tops only, cut into 3-inch pieces and sliced lengthwise

2 celery ribs, sliced very thin (¹/₄- by 4-inch pieces)

1 red bell pepper and 1 yellow bell pepper, trimmed, seeded, and cut into ¹/₄- by 4-inch pieces

2 tablespoons olive oil

Salt and black pepper, to taste

Braciola Stuffed with Vegetables

- Prepare the grill, or preheat the broiler. In a small bowl, whisk together the soy sauce and brown sugar until dissolved.

- Trim and pound the beef tenderloin. Stuff the beef with vegetables, and form it into rolls (see technique for both).

- Grill or broil the beef rolls, brushing with oil to prevent sticking. Grill each roll until it's well browned and the vegetables are hot, about 5 minutes, turning once. The edges of the rolls will begin to curl after about 2½ minutes. Season with salt and pepper.

Braciole Stuffed with Cheese: Prepare the recipe as directed, except omit vegetables. In medium bowl, combine ½ cup grated Parmigiano-Reggiano cheese, 2 beaten eggs, and ½ cup dry Italian flavored bread crumbs. Mix in 2 tablespoons minced fresh basil and 1 tablespoon minced fresh oregano. Spread this mixture on the pounded beef, roll up, and cook as directed.

Braciole with Mushrooms: Prepare the recipe as directed, except omit the green onions, celery, and bell peppers. Cook 1 chopped onion in 2 tablespoons olive oil. Add 1 pound sliced cremini mushrooms and cook until mushrooms are dark and liquid evaporates. Cool 15 minutes, then add 1 cup grated Fontina cheese. Use this mixture to stuff the pounded beef; cook as directed.

Trimming and Stuffing Tenderloin

- Cut the beef tenderloin into eight slices, each approximately ½ inch thick.

- Trim off any fat or connective tissue. You can have your butcher tenderize the meat, or you can do it yourself, using the flat side of a meat mallet to pound each slice to ⅛ inch thick.

- Brush one side of each beef slice with the soy sauce mixture. Sprinkle with salt and pepper.

- Distribute the vegetables equally on each piece of beef. Roll up lengthwise, and skewer each braciola with toothpicks to seal it tightly.

Grilling the Tenderloin

- Brush the tenderloin on each side with a light coat of olive oil to avoid the beef sticking to the grill, then grill beef over direct heat.

- Beef will cook quickly so watch for the edges to curl and remove from heat before the edges become hardened.

- Carefully move the tenderloins off the grill using tongs and season with salt and pepper.

BEEF STEW

Carbonade alla Valdostana is a comforting dish for those cold winter nights around the fireplace

Before refrigeration, beef was only consumed by mountaineers when they had to kill an animal out of necessity. Because they had to preserve the meat to last as long as possible, they cured it with salt, which controls the spoilage of the meat.

The cuisine of Aosta Valley, located near the French Alps in the north of Italy, is simple and substantial as befits a mountain region. Fontina cheese has been produced in Valle d'Aosta since the Middle Ages and is protected by the DOC, which guarantees its quality. The name *carbonade* (from carbone, coal) refers to the thick charcoal-black gravy that forms during the cooking of this stew.

Yield: 4–6 servings

Ingredients:

1 ¹/₂ pounds beef (shoulder meat)

All-purpose flour, as needed

3 ¹/₂ tablespoons butter

1 ¹/₃ pounds onions, chopped

1 bottle strong red wine

Salt and freshly ground pepper

Freshly grated nutmeg, to taste

Beef Stew

- Cut the beef into pieces, dredge in the flour, and pan-fry in butter over high heat in a large skillet.

- Take out the meat and set aside.

- Fry the chopped onions over high heat, add the meat, and simmer gently over low heat. Gradually pour in the wine. Simmer for 2 hours.

- When the meat is ready, season with salt, pepper, and grated nutmeg.

· · · · RECIPE VARIATION · · · ·

Beef Stew with Mushrooms: Prepare the recipe as directed, except add 1 pound cremini or portobello mushrooms, sliced, with the onions. Cook, stirring frequently, until the mushrooms turn dark brown and the liquid is evaporated. Add 2 cups beef broth along with the wine. Simmer the stew for 2 hours, then season with salt, pepper, and nutmeg.

ZOOM

Cooking Meat: Cheaper cuts of meat like round steak, tri-tip, or brisket have more fat and aren't as tender as more expensive cuts. They become meltingly tender, moist, and flavorful when cooked for a long time over low heat. The fat melts and spreads flavor throughout the dish, and the moist cooking environment makes the meat fall off the bone.

Flouring the Beef

- After you cut the beef into large bite-size pieces, dredge it in the flour, shaking off any excess.

- Some cooks like to season their flour with salt and pepper.

- Flour the beef right before you start the cooking process. If done too far in advance, the meat can become gummy or pasty.

Cooking with Wine

- Carbonade is a beef stew cooked with red wine. A strong red wine is recommended.

- The meat will become very tender after simmering for 2 hours in the wine. Check the skillet often to make sure it does not become dry. Add more wine, if necessary.

VEAL CUTLETS WITH FONTINA
This satisfying and fast dish is guaranteed to please even the most finicky kids

Cutlets are usually thin slices of veal loin dipped in bread crumbs and sautéed to a golden brown. Today this specific method has been adopted to include other types of meat such as turkey and chicken, and even vegetables like zucchini and eggplant.

This method was invented by the people of Milan, although the Austrians claim it as originating back when they ruled Italy for about 150 years.

What we can deduce is that the Austrians passed the method of cooking with bread crumbs on to the Italians, who took it to another level, with flour and eggs as the first and second steps and finally the bread crumbs. *Yield: serves 4*

Ingredients:

4 veal chops

3¹/₂ ounces Fontina cheese, sliced

Salt and pepper, to taste

All-purpose flour, as needed

1 egg, beaten

Bread crumbs, as needed

Butter, as needed for frying

Veal Cutlets with Fontina

- Cut a pocket in the veal for the stuffing.

- Fill each of these pockets with some of the Fontina. Press the edges together firmly to seal in the cheese. If necessary, fasten with a toothpick.

- Salt and pepper the veal on both sides. Dredge the veal first in flour, then dip it in the beaten egg, and finally in the bread crumbs.

- In a large pan, fry the veal in butter until golden brown in color.

Chicken Cutlets with Gruyère: Prepare recipe, but substitute 4 boneless, skinless chicken breasts for veal cutlets and substitute 1 cup shredded Gruyère for Fontina. Cut a pocket in the side of each breast and fill with shredded cheese. Season with salt and pepper, then dip in flour, egg, and bread crumbs. Brown in butter for 4 to 5 minutes, turning once, then bake at 350°F for 20 minutes until done.

Pork Cutlets with Gorgonzola: Prepare the recipe as directed, except substitute 8 thin pork cutlets for the veal. Pound the pork until ⅛ inch thick. Top 4 cutlets with 3 tablespoons Gorgonzola cheese and 2 tablespoons diced prosciutto. Cover with remaining cutlets; pound the edges to seal. Coat and cook as directed.

Making a Pocket in Meat

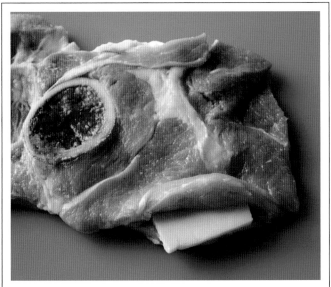

- You will need a very sharp, small knife to make a pocket in each piece of veal.

- To make this step a bit easier, place the veal in the freezer for 30 minutes. Do not allow the meat to freeze completely.

- Place the semi-frozen veal on a cutting board. With one hand, hold the meat in place as you cut into it. Cut at least halfway through, but not all the way, to form the pocket.

Frying Veal Chops

- This recipe calls for shallow frying veal chops in a pan.

- Pan-frying should be done slowly in a small to medium amount of hot fat, in this case butter. This seals in the juices.

- When the bottom sides of the veal chops are golden brown, turn the meat over carefully. Be careful not to burn either side.

- It's always a good idea to let meat come to room temperature before frying.

143

STUFFED GUINEA HEN

The juniper berries in this dish give it a strong, peppery flavor

Guinea fowls are medium-size birds that look like partridges. They produce mostly dark meat and need to be watched closely while cooking: The meat tends to dry out quickly if not basted properly. Because these birds have limited meat, they're served whole and usually stuffed. They are available fresh or frozen usually at butcher's shops. They also are used like chickens for their fresh eggs.

Juniper berries grow wild in the woods on the mountainsides of Italy. Pungent and peppery, they are used commercially to make gin. The process of grinding releases their fragrant and distinctive oils, adding a wonderful flavor to any dish.

Yield: serves 6

Ingredients:

1 whole chicken, about 2 pounds

3 Italian sausages, skin removed

5 sage leaves

1 pinch rosemary

3 garlic cloves

1 teaspoon ground juniper berries

Salt and pepper, to taste

1/4 cup olive oil

1 1/2 cups dry white wine

Sliced lemons, as needed

Stuffed Guinea Hen

- Clean and rinse the chicken; dry it well. In a food processor, combine the sausage meat with the herbs and garlic. Mix in the juniper berries; season with salt and pepper.

- Stuff the chicken. Place it in a casserole with the remaining sausage mixture.

- Place in a preheated 400°F oven for 15 minutes. Add the wine to the casserole. Continue cooking, uncovered, until the chicken is crisp. A meat thermometer inserted into the chicken's thigh should register 160°. Let the chicken rest, covered, for 15 minutes before carving.

Mushroom Stuffed Chicken: Prepare recipe, omitting sausages and juniper berries. Slice ½ pound shiitake and ½ pound cremini mushrooms; cook in 3 tablespoons butter until dark brown. Add 3 minced garlic cloves and cook for 1 minute. Remove from heat and add the minced sage, rosemary, salt, pepper, and 1 cup dried Italian bread crumbs. Stuff the chicken with this mixture; cook as directed.

Risotto Stuffed Chicken: Prepare the recipe as directed, except use 2 to 3 cups cooked risotto in place of the sausages, sage, rosemary, garlic, and juniper berries. Add ½ cup grated Asiago cheese to the risostto and fill the chicken cavity. Season the chicken with salt and pepper and cook as directed.

Stuffing the Chicken

- Before stuffing the chicken, rinse it inside and out under cold running water. Pat dry with paper towels.

- Stuff the chicken with half of the juniper mixture. Do not overstuff. Brush the chicken with olive oil. Sprinkle the outside with salt and pepper.

Grinding Juniper Berries

POULTRY

- Whole spices such as juniper berries can be ground by several methods.

- Specialty cookware stores carry a wide selection of spice mills and graters. You can crack, crush, or crumble your own spices as you need them.

- Grinding can be done in a peppermill or an electric coffee mill. You can also pulverize whole spices with a mortar and pestle.

ROAST CHICKEN W/ONION & CHILE

This is truly a succulent, original, and juicy way of cooking chicken

With its versatility, low cost, and popularity, chicken is a very sought-after item by every food service operation, from elegant restaurants to fast-food chains. Chicken and turkey have become very popular with health-conscious people, too, because poultry has so much less fat and cholesterol than red meats. Italian law requires poultry, like meat, to undergo federal inspections for quality.

When selecting poultry, maturity of the bird is an important consideration. Young, tender birds are more suitable for frying, roasting, and broiling, while older ones are better for dishes that require long cooking. Cooking with wine not only makes tough cuts of meat tender, but also adds lots of extra flavor. This particular dish comes to us from the Marches region of Italy. *Yield: serves 4*

Ingredients:

3–4 tablespoons extra-virgin olive oil

1 small onion, cut into rings

2 garlic cloves, crushed

1 whole chicken, 2–3 pounds, cut into pieces

1 small chile pepper, finely chopped

Salt and freshly ground black pepper

1 tablespoon tomato paste

³/₄ cups dry white wine

A few sprigs of rosemary, with 1 sprig finely chopped

6–8 tablespoons chicken stock (low-sodium)

Roast Chicken with Onion and Chile

- Heat the oil in a casserole; sauté onion rings and crushed garlic for 5 minutes. Add chicken to casserole, followed by chile. Season to taste. Brown chicken on all sides over moderate heat.

- Mix tomato paste with some warm water; add to casserole along with wine. Reduce heat, cover, and cook for approximately 30 minutes.

- Sprinkle chopped rosemary over chicken. Cook for 30 more minutes, or until tender, occasionally adding stock. Garnish with remaining sprigs of rosemary.

Braised Chicken with Artichokes: Prepare the recipe as directed, except omit the chile and tomato paste. When the chicken is browned, add 1 (16-ounce) can drained plain artichoke hearts and 2 cups baby carrots along with 1 cup chicken broth, salt and pepper, wine, and rosemary. Cook the chicken as directed until tender. Serve with vegetables and sauce.

Braised Chicken with Beans: Prepare the recipe as directed, omitting the red chile and tomato paste. Add 1 (14-ounce) can diced tomatoes and 1 teaspoon dried oregano to the pot with the chicken and wine; cover and simmer for 45 minutes. Add 1 pound trimmed fresh green beans and ½ cup olives to the pan; simmer 15 minutes longer.

Browning the Chicken

- You can brown the chicken pieces on all sides by frying them in oil over moderate heat. Frying is a dry-heat method of cooking.

- The degree of browning depends on the temperature level. The higher the heat, the browner the chicken.

Peeling Garlic

- Peeling garlic is easy if you learn a trick or two.

- Smash each garlic clove against a cutting board with the flat side of a heavy kitchen knife. This will loosen the paper-like skin, which you can pull off easily with your fingers.

- Other ways to loosen the skin include pouring hot water over the garlic cloves, soaking the cloves in cool water for 30 minutes, and zapping the cloves for 5 seconds in a microwave oven.

- Use a garlic press for simple crushing.

POTENZA-STYLE CHICKEN

On holidays, Italian kitchens are filled with the aroma of ragu della mamma

Basilicata is a fascinating, tranquil, sun-drenched, reclusive region of Italy, located between the heel and the sole of the Italian boot. It is home of the peperoncino (chile pepper)—a staple of this region's cuisine used in almost every dish. Peperoncini can be found in a variety of shapes and sizes, but they have two common denominators: the red color of their skin, and the fiery hot taste that leaves you gasping for water if you do not eat them with caution.

These chiles belong to the bell pepper family, and usually can be found dried, tied on a string, and hanging from the ceiling in both restaurants and private kitchens for easy picking. They are used in sauces and braised meats. *Yield: serves 4*

Ingredients:

1 chicken, 2³/₄ pounds, whole or cut into pieces

1 can (28–32 ounces) tomatoes

2 tablespoons butter

2 tablespoons olive oil

1 onion, sliced

²/₃ cup dry white wine

1 peperoncino, crushed (chile pepper)

1 tablespoon chopped fresh basil

1 tablespoon chopped fresh parsley

¹/₂ cup crumbled Pecorino Romano cheese

Salt, to taste

Potenza-Style Chicken

- Prepare the chicken and tomatoes (see technique).

- Heat the butter and oil in a large skillet. Add the onion and chicken; brown the chicken pieces on all sides.

- Add the white wine and sprinkle with the peperoncino. As soon as the wine has reduced, add the tomato pieces, basil, parsley, and cheese.

- Cover and cook over low heat for about 1 hour, adding water occasionally if necessary. Season to taste.

Potentina Chicken Breasts: Prepare recipe except substitute 2½ pounds of bone-in, skin-on chicken breasts for the chicken pieces. Brown chicken as directed, then remove from pan. Add white wine and deglaze the pan. Add peperoncino, tomatoes, basil, and parsley; simmer for 20 minutes. Add chicken, simmer for 20 to 30 minutes until tender, and sprinkle with cheese.

About Peperoncini: Any hot chile pepper must be handled with care. When you work with chiles, never touch your face without first thoroughly washing your hands. Using gloves is a good way to avoid spreading the pepper's oils. Pepper seeds and membranes are the hottest parts; for a milder dish, remove those parts.

Prepping Ingredients

- Wash and cut the chicken. Skin, seed, and divide each tomato into eight sections. Rinse the basil and parsley.

- Cut off the basil leaves, and stack them for easy cutting with a large chef's knife.

- The parsley should be chopped with the same knife, first in one direction, and then in the opposite. Repeat this procedure until all the parsley is finely chopped.

Chicken on the Stove

- The chicken in this recipe is cooked in two different ways. First it's browned, and then it's simmered.

- Frying or roasting chicken results in a desirable golden to dark brown exterior.

- Wine and tomatoes are added to the pan, and the chicken continues to cook on a simmer at low heat. Add water if the dish becomes too dry.

POULTRY

CHICKEN SALTIMBOCCA

Pollo Saltimbocca translates as "chicken so good it jumps in your mouth"

Poultry is always cooked well done because birds are carriers of salmonella, which is destroyed by the cooking process.

In order to achieve this, unfortunately, some cooks tend to overcook the meat, thus making it dry and tasteless. Expert chefs can tell when a bird is done simply by how it looks, but the rest of us have to rely on a cooking thermometer. Insert this into the thickest part of the inside of the thigh; it should reach 180°F.

This dish is loved by grown-ups and kids alike. It tastes great and it is easy and fast to make.

Yield: serves 4

KNACK ITALIAN COOKING

Ingredients:

4 boneless chicken breast halves (6 ounces each)

8 thin slices prosciutto

8 medium-size fresh sage leaves

3–4 tablespoons butter, divided

Salt and freshly ground pepper

¹/₂ cup dry white wine

Chicken Saltimbocca

- Prep chicken breasts (see technique). Layer on the ingredients.

- In a large skillet, melt 2 tablespoons of the butter over medium heat. Pan-fry the chicken on each side for about 2 minutes. Season lightly with salt and pepper.

- Remove the chicken from the pan; keep warm.

- Pour the wine into the pan, bring to a boil, and, using a spatula, scrape up the browned bits on the bottom of the pan. Add the rest of butter and stir until melted. Place the chicken back in pan and reheat briefly.

150

Saltimbocca: This word literally translates as "jump in the mouth" or "hop in the mouth." This refers to the flavor of the dish, which explodes with flavor when you bite into it. It can be made with chicken, veal, or even fish. Other ingredients added to the dish include capers, basil, spinach, and prosecco wine. For a creamy finish, you can swirl in another tablespoon of butter before serving.

Veal Saltimbocca: Prepare recipe except substitute four 6-ounce veal cutlets for chicken breasts. Pound veal and top with prosciutto, sage, and ½ cup grated Parmigiano Reggiano cheese. Roll up and cook as directed, but cook veal for 3 to 4 minutes on each side. Omit white wine; use ½ cup Marsala wine instead. Return veal to pan and simmer for 5 to 6 minutes, until done.

Prepping Chicken Breasts

Adding Prosciutto and Sage

POULTRY

- Cut the chicken breasts in half.

- Remove any skin, and place each chicken breast between two large pieces of plastic wrap.

- With a meat mallet (or any other heavy, blunt kitchen implement), pound the chicken breasts until they are flat and even in thickness. This will result in a more tender chicken breast that cooks evenly.

- After the chicken is thoroughly flattened, add the layers of flavor.

- On top of each flattened breast, place a slice of prosciutto and a sage leaf.

- Secure the toppings in place with a toothpick.

DUCK ALLA SCAPPI

This dish was first prepared by a chef to Pope Julius III

Just like chicken, duck needs to be young for frying, broiling, or roasting, and more mature for braising (cooking slowly in a little liquid). Basic cooking for poultry and meat is the same. Turkey, chicken, and veal are so similar that they can be interchanged in most recipes even though to some cooks this might seem unusual. Chili, for example, can be made with chicken or turkey instead of beef, thus cutting the cost in half.

Bartolomeo Scappi was one of the finest chefs of the sixteenth century. His services were requested by the most important people of his time. Pope Julius III appointed Scappi as his personal chef, a position he maintained through the tenures of the next six heads of the Catholic Church. This is one of his recipes, passed on and changed through the years. *Yield: Serves 4–6*

KNACK ITALIAN COOKING

Ingredients:

2 oven-ready wild ducks with giblets (discard the liver)

$^1/_2$ pound cooked ham, cut into small pieces

1 bottle red wine

$^1/_2$ cup red wine vinegar

$2^1/_2$ teaspoons sugar

$^1/_2$ pound pitted plums

$^1/_2$ teaspoon freshly ground white pepper

4 cloves, ground

Ground cinnamon, to taste

Ground nutmeg, to taste

Ground ginger, to taste

1 cup raisins, soaked in lukewarm water

Salt, to taste

Duck alla Scappi

- Prepare the duck (see technique).

- Cover with a lid and bring to a boil on top of the stove. Transfer the casserole to a preheated 350°F oven for about 1 hour or until cooked through.

- Arrange the duck on a warm plate with the plums, and set aside.

- Reduce the sauce in the casserole on top of the stove, and season with salt. Serve the sauce on the side with the meat.

Chicken alla Scappi: Prepare the recipe as directed, except substitute one 4- to 5-pound chicken for the duck. Season the chicken with salt and pepper and place in a casserole with the remaining ingredients. Put directly into a 400°F oven and bake, uncovered, for 55 to 65 minutes, until the chicken is done. Make the sauce as directed; slice the chicken and serve.

ZOOM

About Duck: Duck is very strongly flavored, and its skin contains a lot of fat. As the duck cooks, you may want to skim this fat off the pan from time to time. The fat will float on the surface of the liquid in the casserole. Because duck has such a wild, rather gamy flavor, it is paired with strong ingredients like wine, spices, and dried fruits.

POULTRY

Preparing the Duck

- Clean the ducks and put them in a casserole with all the ingredients except the salt.

- To remove the pit of the plum, cut along the seam all the way through to the pit. Twist the two halves in opposite directions. The pit can then be cut out with ease.

Estimating Measurements

- No measuring cup? No problem. Here are some tips on how to measure food with your eye.

- 1 ounce of cheese is equal to four dice, or the average thumb.

- 3 ounces of meat or fish is equal to a deck of cards.

- 1 cup of fruit salad is equal to a tennis ball.

- 8 ounces of water or milk is equal to a closed hand.

ROASTED CHICKEN W/TOMATOES

This classic Italian dish will quickly become a regular on your menu

Boneless chicken breasts and thin slices of turkey are perfect for sautéing, while larger bone-in pieces take longer to cook. These items are usually browned first by sautéing; you then finish the cooking process in the oven or on the stovetop by simmering the meat in the sauce.

Pan-fried chicken is usually breaded or floured before cooking, to ensure even browning and crispiness. The skin side that will be served faceup on the plate is browned first for the best appearance. You'll need about ¼ inch of oil to pan-fry chicken.

This recipe is so good, you may want to double it so you're sure to have leftovers.

Yield: serves 4

KNACK ITALIAN COOKING

Ingredients:

4 boneless chicken breasts (about 6 ounces each), with skin on

4 fresh bay leaves

¼ teaspoon salt

⅛ teaspoon freshly ground black pepper

2 teaspoons canola oil

2 cups low-sodium chicken broth

1½ pounds tomatoes, sliced ½ inch thick

2 tablespoons balsamic vinegar

Roasted Chicken with Tomatoes

- Prep and brown the chicken breasts (see technique).

- Add the chicken broth to the browned chicken; simmer for 3 to 5 minutes, or until the chicken is cooked through. Remove the chicken from the pan, reserving the broth. Add the tomatoes to the broth (see technique).

- To serve, spoon the tomatoes with sauce into the centers of four plates. Place the chicken breasts over the sauce. Garnish with the reserved bay leaves.

Pan-Roasted Turkey Tenderloins: Prepare the recipe as directed, except substitute 2 boneless, skinless turkey tenderloins for the chicken breasts. Cut the tenderloins in half crosswise to make 4 equal pieces. Do not refrigerate; instead, season the turkey and brown as directed, then simmer with bay leaves, tomatoes, and other ingredients for 15 to 20 minutes until cooked through.

Chicken Thighs with Tomatoes: Prepare the recipe as directed, except substitute 8 skin-on, boneless chicken thighs in place of the chicken breasts. Refrigerate with bay leaves as directed. Brown chicken as directed, but when you add the broth, simmer for 10 to 14 minutes until the chicken is cooked through. Add the tomatoes and continue with the recipe.

Prepping the Chicken Breast

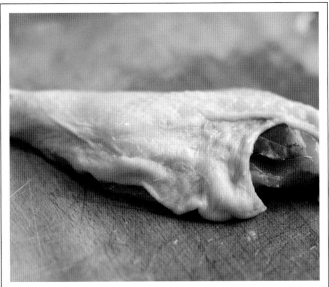

Adding Tomatoes to Broth

POULTRY

- Insert a fresh bay leaf between the skin and meat of each chicken breast.

- Cover and refrigerate for 1 hour. Remove and reserve the bay leaves.

- Heat a large, nonstick sauté pan over medium-low heat until hot. Lightly season each chicken breast with salt and pepper on both sides. Rub oil onto the skin of each breast, and place the breasts skin-side down in the hot sauté pan.

- Turn the heat up to medium, and allow breasts to cook until well browned. Turn the chicken breasts over.

- Add the tomatoes to the chicken broth, and simmer until they are heated through.

- Swirl the pan, rather than stirring, so the tomatoes retain their individual shape and color.

- Remove from the heat immediately, and swirl in the reserved bay leaves.

- Add the balsamic vinegar.

PORK SAUSAGE IN WINE

Pigs in Italy are still raised entirely on natural foods to enhance the flavor of the meat

Pork sausages come in different varieties. The most prized are made with the best cuts of pork meat, fillet, or leg, with all fat removed. The mixture is seasoned with salt, pepper, and fennel seeds, or rendered with pork fat, salt, peperoncini, and fennel seeds. After the sausages are made, they are left to dry for 25 days.

Pork has always been popular in Friuli-Venezia Giulia, a small region located in the very north of Italy near the Austrian border. There it is still the custom for many families to rear their own pigs. Sauris is a very small town in Friuli famous for its sausages and ham. Customers often travel long distance to buy these specialties. *Yield: serves 2*

Ingredients:

4 salsicce (sausages)

1 tablespoons white wine vinegar

³/₄ cup white wine

Pork Sausage in Wine

- Prick the sausages a few times all over.

- In a frying pan, begin to cook them over medium-low heat, and sprinkle them with the white wine vinegar.

- When this has been absorbed, pour on the wine and continue cooking for about 10 minutes.

Grilled Salsicce: Prick the sausages all over and place them in the pan with the vinegar and wine. Simmer the sausages over low heat for 8 to 9 minutes until firm, then transfer them to a prepared and heated grill. Grill, turning frequently with tongs, until the sausages are thoroughly cooked, crisp and golden brown, about 8 to 10 minutes.

Grilled Onions: Grilled onions are a great accompaniment to sausages. Peel 3 large yellow onions and slice them ¾ inch thick. Pierce with a skewer side-to-side to hold the slices together. Brush with 2 tablespoons olive oil and sprinkle with salt and pepper. Grill, turning once, until golden and tender, about 8 to 11 minutes. Remove the skewers and serve with sausages.

Preparing the Sausages

- With a fork or the tip of a sharp knife, poke a few holes in each sausage.

- Turn the sausages over and repeat.

- This will allow some of the fat inside the sausage casing to render out into the frying pan.

Cooking with Wine

- These sausages are flavorful in their own right, but adding wine to the frying pan gives them a whole new level of taste.

- Avoid using bottled "cooking" wines. Instead, use a wine that you would enjoy drinking with this particular dish.

- The recipe calls for white wine, but you also might want to try it with a red.

PORK/HAM

ROAST LEG OF PORK IN MILK

Milan is known for delicious, wholesome meals, and this dish is no exception

The slaughtering of the pig is a family affair and a very important event in Italy—so much so that this is celebrated throughout the nation with big parties.

There are several breeds of pigs in Italy, and a few are on the threshold of extinction. One of the endangered species is the Cinta Senese, which originally came from Siena. This type

of pig can't be kept in pigsties because it gains too much weight too fast and thus retains too much water. Instead it's allowed to freely roam the hills, feeding on acorns, beechnuts, fruits, and berries, yielding sweet, flavorful, and aromatic meat products. Unfortunately, this practice has become too expensive for breeders to maintain. *Yield: serves 4–6*

Ingredients:

Generous 2-pound leg of pork

1 garlic clove

2 cups dry white wine

All-purpose flour, as needed

3¹/₂ tablespoons butter

1 sprig rosemary, chopped

3 cups milk

Salt and freshly ground black pepper

Roast Leg of Pork in Milk

- Marinate meat in garlic and wine. Carefully pat it dry, and dust lightly with flour.

- Heat butter in a large pan, add rosemary, and brown meat on all sides.

- Pour on milk, and season with salt and pepper. Cover and braise for 2 hours, or

until tender.

- Place meat in a warmed dish, and keep it hot. Boil cooking liquid until it has reduced to a creamy consistency.

- Slice meat and serve hot with sauce poured over it.

Milk-Braised Pork Roast: Prepare the recipe as directed, except substitute a 2-pound pork roast for the leg of pork. Cut 2 garlic cloves into slivers. Pierce the pork all over with a sharp knife and insert the garlic slivers deeply into the pork. Season well, dust with flour, and brown in butter with the rosemary. Braise for 1½ to 2 hours until the milk has reduced and the pork is cooked.

Milk-Braised Veal: Prepare recipe as directed, except use a 2-pound veal roast in place of the leg of pork. Rub the veal with a split garlic clove, season with salt and pepper, and dust with flour. Brown in 2 tablespoons butter and 1 tablespoon olive oil. Add the onions to the pot and cook until tender, then add rosemary and milk. Simmer for 1½ hours, until done.

Prepping the Meat

Braising

- Place the meat in a large pan.

- Slice the garlic, and sprinkle it over the meat. Some cooks like to insert the sliced garlic into slits they've cut into the meat.

- Pour the wine into the pan. Cover the pan, and marinate the meat for 2 days in the refrigerator.

- Braising results in a moist, flavorful dish that is incredibly tender.

- Braising can be done with a variety of liquids, from stocks to wine to milk. The secret is to use a small amount of liquid so that the meat is braised, not boiled.

- The braising must take place in a tightly closed pan, just large enough to hold the meat.

PORK/HAM

PORK IN BALSAMIC VINEGAR

Porchetta is grilled on an open spit until the skin crackles

Every part of the pig, even blood and organ meat, is used to prepare sausages and other pork products in Italy. The blood and organs are mixed with raisins and pine nuts to make Italy's famous sanguinaccio (blood pudding).

Musetto (little snout) is a pork sausage that includes the finely ground snout of the pig, and the mixture is then flavored with white wine.

Umbria in central Italy is famous for its porchetta or roast suckling pig, grilled on an open spit with fresh rosemary until the skin crackles and is almost bronze in color. This dish is very easy to prepare, and it can be cooked up to three days ahead. The marinade, which includes balsamic vinegar, gives the pork a flavor that is hard to beat.

Yield: serves 4

Ingredients:

Marinade:

1 medium white onion, thinly sliced

¹/₄ cup cider vinegar

3 tablespoons fresh rosemary

2 tablespoons minced fresh sage

1 tablespoon chopped fresh parsley

²/₃ cup balsamic vinegar

Juice of ¹/₂ lemon

1 tablespoon pink peppercorns

¹/₂ cup extra-virgin olive oil

Pork:

1¹/₂ pounds boneless pork tenderloin

2 tablespoons olive oil, divided

Salt and pepper, to taste

²/₃ cup dry white wine

Pork in Balsamic Vinegar

- Prepare the marinade (see technique). Preheat the oven to 375°F.

- Pat the meat dry with paper towels, and rub it with 1 tablespoon of the olive oil; sprinkle with salt and black pepper.

- Marinate the meat, and then roast it (see technique).

- Bring the meat and the pan juices to room temperature before serving. Cut it into thin slices, arrange on a serving dish, and spoon some of the juices over the slices.

Roasted Porchetta: Rather than cooking meat in marinade and then chilling it, prepare marinade, reducing olive oil to ¼ cup. Add raw meat. Cover and refrigerate for 8 to 24 hours. Drain meat and pat dry, reserving marinade. Brown meat and roast as directed. Bring marinade to a boil; cook for 5 to 10 minutes until reduced. Swirl in 2 tablespoons butter. Serve with hot sliced pork.

ZOOM

How to Brown Meat: As meat browns, its proteins and sugars break down and recombine to form hundreds of complex compounds that create a caramelized flavor. There are three rules for browning meat correctly. The meat should be patted dry, the pan must be hot, and don't turn the meat until it releases easily. If the meat is wet or the pan cool, the meat will steam, not brown.

Preparing the Marinade

- To make the marinade, in a skillet, combine the onion and cider vinegar, and simmer until the onion is soft.

- Add the rosemary, sage, parsley, balsamic vinegar, lemon juice, peppercorns, and extra-virgin olive oil. Stir well; remove from the heat, and set aside.

- Transfer the meat to a deep nonmetal dish just large enough to hold it. Pour the marinade over the meat and let it marinate, covered, in the refrigerator for at least 3 hours or up to 3 days.

Browning and Roasting

- In a large frying pan, heat the remaining olive oil over medium-high heat, and brown the meat on all sides.

- Transfer the meat to a baking dish, and add ⅓ cup of the wine to the dish.

- Roast for 20 to 25 minutes, or until the meat reaches 155° to 160°F on a meat thermometer.

- Midway through the cooking, add the remaining ⅓ cup wine to the pan.

MEATBALLS WITH FONTINA

This is a popular dish in Italy—the pork and cheese together give it a rich flavor

The delicious Italian ham known as prosciutto comes from Parma. This cured meat is controlled by DOC, which means that its origin is legally protected and monitored. The pigs' diet and growth are also controlled by the consortium. The extra-special flavor of the prosciutto is mostly attributed to the ham makers' skills. The pigs are slaughtered at the age of ten months, and only after they reach 300 pounds. The hams are then hung to dry for fourteen months.

These meatballs are perfect to stuff with nuggets of creamy cheese that melt during cooking. In this particular dish, the meatballs are filled with Fontina cheese cubes, then rolled in bread crumbs and sautéed. *Yield: serves 6–8*

Ingredients:

1¼ pounds lean ground pork

1¼ pounds lean ground beef

3 garlic cloves, crushed

Grated rind and juice of 1 lemon

2 slices day-old bread, cubed

½ cup grated Parmigiano Reggiano cheese

½ teaspoon ground cinnamon

1 teaspoon dried oregano

2 eggs, beaten

1 teaspoon salt

Ground black pepper

5 ounces Fontina cheese, cut into 16 cubes

1¼ cups dry plain bread crumbs

Olive oil, as needed for frying

Meatballs with Fontina

- Preheat the oven to 350°F. Mix the ingredients for meatballs, and form into 16 meatballs.

- Add cheese to each (see technique).

- Roll the meatballs in the bread crumbs. Heat the olive oil in a large frying pan. Cook the meatballs in batches until they are lightly browned on all sides.

- Transfer to a roasting pan and bake for 20 minutes, or until cooked through. Garnish with fresh basil and more grated cheese, and serve with cooked pasta and tomato sauce.

···· RECIPE VARIATIONS ····

Light Meatballs: Prepare the recipe as directed, except use ¾ pound each lean ground pork and ground beef, and add 1 pound ground veal. Omit the cinnamon and oregano; add 1 teaspoon each dried basil and dried thyme. Replace the Fontina with cubes of mozzarella cheese. Make the meatballs, fill, cook, and serve as directed.

Classic Meatballs: Prepare recipe except cook ⅓ cup finely minced onion and 2 minced garlic cloves in 2 tablespoons olive oil. Remove to a bowl and add crumbled bread, Parmigiano Reggiano, oregano, eggs, salt, and 1 cup grated Asiago cheese. Form into meatballs, but do not stuff with cheese or roll in bread crumbs. Cook as directed and serve with pasta and sauce. Sprinkle with more Asiago cheese.

Mixing Meatball Ingredients

Stuffing Meatballs

- In a large bowl, combine the ground pork and beef with the garlic, lemon rind, lemon juice, fresh bread crumbs, grated cheese, cinnamon, and oregano.

- Sir in the beaten eggs; mix well. Add the salt and a generous pinch of the black pepper.

- Using clean hands occasionally dipped into cold water, knead the mixture to ensure that all the ingredients are evenly distributed. Form 16 meatballs of equal size.

- Cup each meatball in one hand, and press a cube of Fontina into the center.

- Reshape the meatball, making sure the cheese is well enclosed in the meat. You want the cheese to stay inside the meatball rather than oozing out.

163

PORK W/SMOKED CHEESE SAUCE

Sheep's-milk cheeses melted with cream make a simple and luxurious sauce

Pork must be cooked long enough to eliminate the danger of a disease called trichinosis, caused by a parasite that lives in the muscle tissue and is killed at 137°F. To be safe, pork should be cooked to at least 150° to 155°F. At this stage, pork is cooked medium to medium-well. Remove it from the heat and let it rest, covered, for 10 to 15 minutes before serving.

The meat will continue cooking in pan.

To determine the right temperature, an instant thermometer is essential. This can be inserted into the meat at any time while it's cooking. Veal and pork when cooked change color from pink and gray-pink to white or off-white.
Yield: serves 4

KNACK ITALIAN COOKING

Ingredients:

8 small to medium-size pork chops

2 tablespoons butter, divided

1 tablespoon extra-virgin olive oil

Salt and black pepper

2 garlic cloves, crushed

2$^1/_2$ cups button mushrooms, sliced

1 cup frozen peas

$^1/_4$ cup brandy

1 cup heavy cream

5 ounces smoked sheep's-milk cheese (Manchego or Idiazabal, available in most supermarkets), diced

Italian flat-leaf parsley, for garnish

Pork with Smoked Cheese Sauce

- Sauté the chops in butter and oil (see technique). The cooked chops should feel firm to the touch, with a very light springiness.

- Remove the chops to a serving dish; keep hot. Add the remaining butter to the pan. Stir-fry the garlic and mushrooms for 3 minutes.

- Add the peas and brandy; cook until the pan juices have been absorbed.

- Season lightly. Using a slotted spoon, place mushrooms and peas on top of chops. Add cheese to sauce in pan. Pour sauce over chops, garnishing with parsley.

Veal Chops with Smoked Cheese Sauce: Prepare recipe except substitute 8 veal chops for the pork chops. Omit button mushrooms; use cremini instead. Coat veal chops with flour seasoned with salt and pepper, then brown for 3 to 4 minutes on each side. Add ½ cup beef broth; simmer chops, covered, for 15 to 20 minutes, until they reach 150°F. Remove from pan and proceed with recipe.

Pork Chops with Tomato Sauce: Prepare recipe but add 1 chopped onion to pan after chops have been browned. Omit mushrooms; add 4 peeled and chopped red tomatoes. Replace brandy with ¼ cup dry red wine. Cook tomatoes until they soften and break down, about 10 minutes. Add cream and chops, then bring to a simmer. Stir in ⅓ cup grated Parmesan cheese instead of smoked cheese.

Sautéing the Meat

Making the Cheese Sauce

- Melt half the butter with the oil in a large heavy-bottomed frying pan.

- Season the chops with salt and pepper, and brown them on each side in batches over medium-high heat.

- Reduce the heat, and cook for about 7 minutes on each side until just done.

- Pour the heavy cream into the frying pan, and mix well.

- Stir in the diced cheese.

- Over medium-low heat, stir constantly until the cheese has melted.

- Season with pepper only. The cheese adds enough salt to flavor the sauce.

PORK/HAM

SCALLOPS WRAPPED IN PROSCIUTTO

Cook these skewers on the grill for alfresco summer dining

Scallops are part of the shellfish family. There are two kinds of scallops:

Bay scallops are small with a delicate taste and texture. They're very expensive; expect to get 34 to 35 per pound.

Sea scallops are less delicate, but still tender (unless they're overcooked); expect to get 10 to 15 per pound.

Scallops are available all year long, are creamy white in color, and have a sweet flavor, which is a sign of freshness.

Scallops do not need anything added to improve their flavor. The most popular cooking methods are sautéing, poaching, deep-frying, and broiling.

This mouthwatering recipe calls for prosciutto, imported from the Italian city of Parma. Prosciutto is ham cured without smoke and sliced paper-thin. *Yield: serves 4*

Ingredients:

24 medium-size scallops

Lemon juice

12 prosciutto slices, each cut lengthwise into 2 strips

Olive oil, as needed for brushing

Ground black paper, to taste

Lemon wedges, as needed for serving

Scallops Wrapped in Prosciutto

- Prepare grill or preheat broiler.

- Sprinkle scallops with lemon juice. Wrap a strip of prosciutto around each scallop. Thread onto eight skewers, three scallops per skewer.

- Brush with oil. Arrange on a baking sheet if you'll be broiling. Broil about 4 inches from the heat, or cook on the grill, for 3 to 4 minutes on each side, or until scallops are opaque.

- Sprinkle the scallops with freshly ground black pepper, and serve with lemon wedges.

Scallops are a tasty and easy-to-use low-fat food. They come prepared, without their shell, packed in their liquor. There may be a small muscle attached to the side of each scallop; you can feel it with your fingers. Just pull it off and discard before using the scallops, because this muscle can be tough when cooked. Use scallops within a day or two of purchase.

Shrimp Wrapped in Prosciutto: Prepare recipe except substitute 24 large shrimp for scallops. Rinse the shrimp, remove their shells, then cut a slit along the back of each and rinse out the dark vein. Sprinkle with lemon juice, wrap in prosciutto, then proceed with the recipe as directed. The shrimp should cook for 2 to 4 minutes on each side until they curl and turn pink.

Wrapping the Scallops

Soaking Skewers

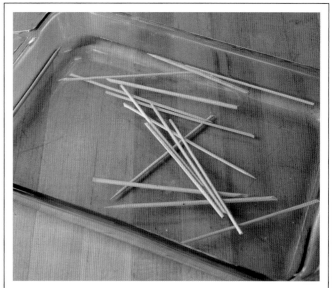

PORK/HAM

- By cutting the 12 slices of prosciutto in half lengthwise, you will end up with 24 slices, enough to wrap around the 24 scallops.

- Because the prosciutto is sliced paper-thin, and

because of its texture, it is very easy to wrap each scallop with a long piece.

- Toothpicks are not needed to secure the prosciutto, which clings nicely to itself.

- If you're using wooden, not metal skewers, soak them in water for 20 minutes before you load them with the scallops.

- This is to prevent the skewers from catching on fire when placed on the grill.

- If you are using metal skewers, be very careful: The entire skewer becomes very hot to the touch.

167

FISH IN PARCHMENT PAPER

This method of cooking fish is impressive, easy, and fast

Fish and shellfish are the most perishable of all foods. Storing them properly is essential, and cooking them as soon as possible is of the uttmost priority. The fishy taste that people hate is actually a sign of spoilage. Fish should taste sweet and fresh.

Fresh fish is not inspected by federal law, so it's very important that you examine it carefully before you purchase.

Wrapping the fish in parchment paper for cooking keeps it moist and captures the tasty juices. Paper-thin slices of vegetables are cooked along with the fish, giving you a complete meal with no cleanup. This dish is impressive enough for company. Any firm-fleshed white fish such as cod, haddock, or catfish will do.

Yield: serves 4–6

Ingredients:

Parchment paper or aluminum foil

3 tablespoons olive oil, divided

4 cups spinach, rinsed and well drained

2¹/₂ pounds fish fillets

2–3 fennel sprigs

1 onion, sliced paper-thin

1 carrot, sliced paper-thin

¹/₂ fennel bulb, sliced paper-thin

¹/₂ cup dried tomatoes packed in oil, drained and diced

Salt and black pepper, to taste

Fish in Parchment Paper

- Preheat the oven to 450°F.

- Place a large sheet of parchment paper or aluminum foil on a baking sheet large enough to hold all the fish. Brush with 1 tablespoon of oil.

- Arrange the fish and the vegetables (see technique).

- Enclose the fish and the vegetables (see technique).

- Bake the fish for 10 to 12 minutes. Carefully transfer the packet of fish to a serving dish. Open up the parchment or foil. Serve the fish with vegetables and juices spooned over.

Grilled Fish in Foil: Prepare the recipe as directed, except use a very large sheet of heavy-duty aluminum foil instead of the parchment paper. Wrap using double folds, and leave some space in the package for air expansion as the food cooks. Place over hot coals, close the cover, and grill for 10 to 12 minutes, arranging occasionally. Be careful of steam when opening the packets to serve.

Individual Fish in Parchment Paper: Prepare recipe except divide all ingredients into six equal portions. Tear off smaller pieces of parchment paper or heavy-duty aluminum foil. Assemble each packet as directed and wrap using a double fold. Bake or grill packets for 10 to 12 minutes until fish flakes when tested with a fork. Place each on an individual plate. Warn diners to open packets carefully.

Arranging the Fish and Vegetables

- In the center of the oiled parchment or foil, make a bed of the spinach. Place all the fish on top of the spinach.

- Place the fennel sprigs atop the fish. Scatter the sliced onions, carrots, fennel bulb, and diced dried tomatoes over all the fish.

- Sprinkle with remaining oil, salt, and pepper.

Folding the Parchment or Foil

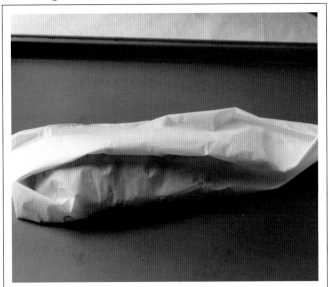

- When all the fish and vegetables are arranged in the center of the parchment or foil, it's time to turn it into one large sealed packet.

- Bring the four sides of the parchment or foil up and over the ingredients. Fold the edges together to make a seal. This is very easy to do with foil.

- With parchment paper, you can fasten the edges with paper clips.

FISH

FISH IN SAFFRON CREAM SAUCE

This meal is perfect for a quiet evening at home with that special someone

There are a lot of varieties of fish consumed around the world, but few are as popular as flounder with its fine flakes, white flesh, and sweet flavor. Winter flounder, lemon sole, and gray sole are all available and all lean.

After you buy fish and before you use it, be sure to wrap it or keep it in its original moisture-proof container. Fresh fish can be stored in the refrigerator for two days. If you want to keep it for longer than this, freeze it, or cook it before storing.

Fresh fish should be stored in the refrigerator on crushed ice, with a drip pan underneath so the melting ice can drain. Change the ice daily. Keep the fish covered and stored away from other foods. *Yield: serves 4*

KNACK ITALIAN COOKING

Ingredients:

1 1/2 pounds sole or flounder fillets

3-4 tablespoons fresh lemon juice, divided

Salt and freshly ground pepper

1 tablespoon butter

2 shallots, peeled and minced

1 1/4 cups fish stock

1/2 cup heavy cream

1/8-1/4 teaspoon crumbled saffron threads (available in any specialty food store)

2-3 tablespoons water

Fish in Saffron Cream Sauce

- Prepare the fish (see technique).

- Cook the fish in a large skillet (see technique).

- Stir the cream into the skillet. Dissolve the saffron in water; add to the skillet. Let the sauce cook for 30 minutes, or until very creamy.

- Season with salt, pepper, and the remaining lemon juice. Lay the fish in the hot sauce to heat through before serving.

Fish Fillets in Herbed Cream Sauce: Prepare recipe, except substitute 1 small minced onion and 1 minced garlic clove for the shallots. Omit saffron and add 1 tablespoon each fresh minced thyme, mint, and basil. Or you can use 1 teaspoon each dried thyme and basil, and ½ teaspoon dried mint leaves. Other herb combinations are also good, including Herbes de Provence, or oregano and thyme.

Fish Fillets in Curry Sauce: Prepare recipe, except in place of saffron use 2–3 teaspoons curry powder and ½ teaspoon turmeric. Turmeric is an inexpensive substitute for saffron. Add 2 cloves minced garlic to pan along with shallots and cook until tender, then add stock, cream, and curry powder. Simmer sauce as directed, then add fish and heat.

Preparing the Fish

- Drizzle the fillets with 2 tablespoons of the lemon juice; season with salt and pepper.

- In a large skillet, melt the butter over medium heat. Sauté shallots until translucent.

- Add the stock to the pan, bring to a boil, and reduce to a simmer.

Cooking in Batches

- Place half of the fish fillets in the skillet containing the simmering broth. Cover and cook for 2 to 3 minutes.

- Transfer the fish to a warmed serving dish; cover to keep warm.

- Sauté the rest of fish in the same way, and keep warm.

FISH

PEPPERED FISH

This delightful dish gets its name from the more mild flavored green peppercorns

When fish is cooked, the flesh flakes or comes apart. Even after it's removed from the heat, however, fish continues cooking. If you're not careful, by the time the dish reaches the table it could already be dry and overcooked.

There are various tests to determine doneness when you're cooking fish: If the fish is beginning to flake but not yet falling apart, it's ready. For boned fish, if you see the flesh separating from the bone, and the bone itself is no longer pink, it's done. If the flesh has turned from translucent to opaque (usually white), the fish is good to go.

Yield: serves 8

Ingredients:

8 fish fillets, about 6 ounces each (rockfish, cod, halibut, or sea bass)

4 garlic cloves, peeled and minced

Juice from $1/2$ lemon

Salt and freshly ground pepper

$1/2$ cup (1 stick) butter, softened

3 tablespoons brandy

1 tablespoon green peppercorns, drained

$1/4$ cup olive oil

$1/2$ cup bread crumbs

Lemon slices, for garnish

Peppered Fish

- Sprinkle the fish with the garlic and lemon juice. Season with salt and pepper.

- Preheat the oven to 400°F.

- In a bowl, mix the butter with the brandy and peppercorns; season with salt and pepper.

- Bake the fish on a preheated baking sheet (see technique).

- Turn the fish over. Scatter bread crumbs and little dabs of flavored butter over each fillet. Bake the fish for another 6 to 8 minutes, or until cooked through. Garnish with lemon slices.

Crisp Peppered Fish: Prepare the recipe as directed, except instead of using plain bread crumbs to cover the fish, substitute panko, or Japanese bread crumbs. These crumbs are very light and crisp and can be found in the international foods aisle of the supermarket. You can also substitute crushed crisp cereal.

ZOOM

Green peppercorns are picked and dried while the berry is immature. This gives the pepper a fruity and lighter taste that isn't as hot as black or white peppercorns. You can also find pink and rainbow peppercorns on the market. Try them before adding them to the dishes you make. Or combine several colors to make your own unique blend.

Preheat the Baking Sheet

- This recipe is a little unusual in that you need to preheat the baking sheet for the fish.

- Brush the baking sheet with oil, and place it in the oven to preheat.

- When the sheet is hot, lay the fish on it in a single layer. Bake for about 5 minutes.

- Turn the fish over. Scatter bread crumbs and flavored butter over each fillet. Bake the fish for another 6 to 8 minutes, or until it's cooked through.

Mincing Garlic

- Smash each garlic clove with the flat side of a heavy chef knife. This will loosen the paper skin for easy removal.

- Use a garlic press, if you have one, to finely mince the garlic.

- Or you can use a very sharp knife to slice each clove as thin as possible, and then finely chop until the garlic is minced. Adding a pinch of salt makes this easier.

FISH

173

SALMON WITH SWEET PEPPER SAUCE

Grown-ups are as eager for this delicacy as children on Christmas Day

Salmon can be classified as either saltwater or freshwater fish, because they live in the ocean but swim up rivers to spawn. Although it's high in fat, this is a good fat that helps clean your arteries just like olive oil.

Salmon has pink to red flesh with a meaty texture and flavor. It is very expensive. Atlantic, chinook, sockeye, coho, chum, and humpback are among the varieties, although the

Atlantic salmon is the most recognizable. Some salmon is farm raised.

The fat protects the fish from drying out while cooking, which means this fish is best suited for broiling and baking. The dry heat from the oven helps eliminate some of its extra oil.

Yield: serves 4

Ingredients:

Sweet Pepper Sauce:

2 red bell peppers, roasted, peeled, and seeded (available by the jar in supermarkets)

2 garlic cloves, chopped finely

3 tablespoons freshly squeezed lemon juice

¹/₂ cup low-fat mayonnaise

1 pinch cayenne pepper

1 teaspoon chili powder

1 teaspoon honey

2 tablespoons olive oil

2 tablespoons freshly ground black pepper

4 (6-ounce) salmon steaks

Salmon with Sweet Pepper Sauce

- Preheat the broiler.

- Make the Sweet Pepper Sauce (see technique).

- Pour the oil onto a plate. Place the black pepper on another plate. Dip the salmon in the oil, then press it into the pepper.

- Broil the salmon, turning once after 4 minutes for medium-rare. When the salmon sweats, the fish is done.

- Serve with Sweet Pepper Sauce for dipping on the side, approximately 2 tablespoons per serving.

Tuna with Sweet Pepper Sauce: Prepare the recipe as directed, except substitute four 6-ounce tuna steaks for the salmon steaks. Coat the steaks in the oil and black pepper and cook as directed. Tuna can be served medium-rare if you are sure it's fresh from an impeccable source. Or cook it until the flesh flakes, or is well done.

Salmon with Spicy Pepper Sauce: Prepare the recipe as directed, but substitute 1 poblano pepper, 1 jalapeño pepper, and 1 yellow bell pepper for the roasted red bell peppers. Cut each pepper in half, remove the seeds, and roast over a gas flame until the skin is blackened. Place in a bag and steam for 10 minutes, then remove the skin. Make the sauce and cook the fish as directed.

Making the Sweet Pepper Sauce

- In a food processor or blender, combine the peppers, garlic, lemon juice, mayonnaise, cayenne pepper, chili powder, and honey.

- Mix on high speed for 30 seconds or with a hand blender for 1 to 2 minutes until blended well.

- Set aside.

Coating the Salmon

- To coat the salmon steaks, set up two plates.

- Pour the olive oil into one plate, and place the pepper on the other.

- First dip each salmon steak in the oil, then press it into the pepper. The salmon will be evenly coated with black pepper. If it's easier, you can also brush the salmon with oil instead of dipping it.

FISH

FISH WITH LEMON-CAPER BUTTER

This is one of the best fish dishes I have eaten in Italy

Capers are tiny unopened flower buds of a bush found near the Mediterranean. This bush grows freely in dry, stony soil along the Italian caost. After being harvested in the spring, the buds need to be prepared for eating. The tinier the buds, the better the taste.

To eliminate their bitterness, they are preserved in a brine solution, or placed in vinegar for several days. Either method helps the buds last a very long time.

Before using, the capers must be rinsed to eliminate the salt or the strong vinegar taste. A few added to a salad, tomato sauce, vegetable, or fish dish can make all the difference. Glass jars of capers can be found in supermarkets. This is a tangy dish.

Yield: serves 4

Ingredients:

1 1/2 pounds fish fillets (cod, rockfish, or halibut)

3 tablespoons all-purpose flour

1-2 tablespoons olive oil

Sauce:

Juice and zest from 1 lemon

2-4 tablespoons (1/4-1/2 stick) cold butter

1 tablespoon drained and rinsed capers

1/2 bunch fresh Italian parsley, finely chopped

Salt and freshly ground pepper

Fish with Lemon-Caper Butter

- Coat the fish fillets with flour, shaking off the excess.

- Lay the fillets in a hot pan containing oil; pan-fry for 1 minute. Reduce the heat to low; carefully turn the fillets and fry for 2 to 4 minutes more, or until the fish is no longer translucent.

- Remove the fish from the pan; cover and keep warm.

- Pour the oil out of the pan, and make the sauce (see technique).

- Put the fillets back in the pan with the sauce to reheat.

Fish Fillets with Fried Capers: Prepare the recipe as directed, but before you pour the oil out of the pan, drop in the drained capers. Be careful; they will spatter. Fry until the capers open and become crisp; remove them from the oil and drain on paper towels. Continue with the recipe, garnishing the fish with the fried capers.

Fish with Citrus-Caper Butter: Prepare the recipe as directed, except cook 1 minced garlic clove in the pan before adding the butter. Substitute 1 tablespoon each lemon juice, orange juice, and grapefruit juice for the whole lemon. Add ½ teaspoon of each fruit's zest to the finished sauce. Garnish the dish with finely minced fresh basil leaves.

Flouring the Fish

- In a large nonstick frying pan, heat the olive oil over medium-high heat.

- Put the flour on a large flat plate. Lay each fish fillet in the flour, and coat both sides of the fish evenly. Shake off the excess flour before adding the fish to the hot pan.

Making the Sauce

- Lightly wipe the oil out of the pan in which you fried the fish.

- Add the lemon juice and, with a wooden spoon, stir in small dabs of the cold butter.

- Mix in the lemon zest, capers, and parsley. Season with salt and pepper.

FISH

TUNA WITH MUSHROOM SAUCE

The tarragon in this sauce creates an irresistible scent

If you are one of those people who is under the impression that tuna in a can is all there is, this is a good time to try this dish. Tuna has a meaty texture and is a fat type of fish. The belly contains more fat than the back ("loin"). The red flesh variety is used for sushi. Some other varieties are also available.

Tuna usually is cut into steaks and grilled. It should be cooked medium-rare, or it will dry out.

This is a scrumptious dish flavored with tarragon, which has a distinctive aniseed flavor that is good with fish, cream, and mushrooms. In this recipe, oyster mushrooms provide both texture and flavor.

Yield: serves 4

Ingredients:

4 tuna steaks, 6 ounces each

Salt and cayenne pepper

$1/4$ cup ($1/2$ stick) unsalted butter

1 shallot, finely chopped

6 ounces assorted mushrooms, trimmed and sliced

1 cup chicken or vegetable stock (low-sodium)

2 teaspoons cornstarch

$1/2$ teaspoon prepared mustard

$1/4$ cup heavy cream

3 tablespoons chopped fresh tarragon

1 teaspoon white wine vinegar

Tuna with Mushroom Sauce

- Season the tuna steaks with salt and cayenne pepper.

- In a large frying pan, cook the tuna in melted butter (see technique). Set the cooked fish aside.

- In the same pan, make the Tarragon Mushroom Sauce (see technique).

- Spoon sauce over each tuna steak.

Salmon with Tarragon Sauce: Prepare the recipe as directed, except substitute four 6-ounce salmon steaks for the tuna steaks. Cook the salmon for 8 to 9 minutes, turning once; the center should still be red and translucent. Set the salmon aside, covered, to rest while you make the sauce. Make the sauce as directed, replacing the regular mustard with 2 teaspoons Dijon mustard .

Tuna with Tarragon Tomato Sauce: Prepare the recipe as directed, omitting the mushrooms. Add 7 chopped red plum tomatoes to the dish and cook for 4 minutes, then add the stock and cook on low heat until the tomatoes soften and start to break apart. Continue with the recipe, adding the fish back to the sauce to heat through 1 or 2 minutes before serving.

Cooking the Tuna

- Cook the tuna in the melted butter for 5 minutes, turning once.

- Transfer the cooked tuna to a plate; cover and keep warm.

- Use the same pan to make the Mushroom Tarragon Sauce.

Making the Sauce

- In the same frying pan in which you cooked the tuna steaks, heat the remaining butter and fry the shallot until soft.

- Add the mushrooms; cook until their juices begin to flow. Add the stock and simmer for 2 to 3 minutes.

- Combine the cornstarch and mustard; blend with 1 tablespoon of water. Stir into the mushroom mixture. Bring to a simmer, stirring to thicken.

- Add the cream, tarragon, and vinegar. Season to taste; simmer for 3 more minutes.

FISH

179

SEAFOOD SALAD

Sweet scallops, crunchy shrimp, and chewy squid make an incredible combination

If someone asked me the single most outstanding characteristic of Italian food, I would have to say freshness. A successful seafood dish depends very much on this factor. The size of the squid (they should be very small here) and the cooking time (do not overcook them) are very important as well.

Squid are classified as mollusks even though they have no shell. They must be skinned and eviscerated, with the head and back discarded. The body and tentacles are eaten. Squid are cut up and either fried quickly (5 to 7 minutes) or simmered in liquid for 45 minutes. Already cleaned squid can be purchased at any fish market or in the fish section of any supermarket. *Yield: serves 8*

Ingredients:

Marinade:

Juice of 2–3 lemons (more or less to taste)

$^1/_2$ cup extra-virgin olive oil

3 garlic cloves, peeled and crushed

$^1/_4$ cup chopped fresh parsley

$^1/_3$ cup chopped fresh fennel leaves

$^1/_2$ cup diced red bell peppers

2 tablespoons red wine vinegar

1 teaspoon salt (more or less to taste)

Coarsely ground black pepper, to taste

$^1/_2$ pound medium-size shrimp, peeled and deveined

1 pound bay scallops

2 pounds small squid

Seafood Salad

- Make the marinade and prepare the seafood.

- Add shrimp to boiling salted water and simmer until pink, about 3 minutes. Remove with a slotted spoon and cool. Repeat with the scallops.

- Add squid rings to hot water; simmer until tender, 12 to 20 minutes. About 5 minutes before they're done, add diced tentacles.

- Drain well. Add cooked seafood to marinade; toss, cover, and refrigerate for 2 to 3 hours, turning frequently. Serve at room temperature.

When you buy seafood, use your nose! Fresh seafood should always smell mild, sweet, and slightly salty, like the sea. It should never smell fishy, musty, or strong. Fresh fish, purchased whole, should look moist with tight skin and round eyes. Shrimp and scallops should smell sweet. Use fresh seafood within a day or two of purchase, or freeze it for longer storage.

···· **RECIPE VARIATION** ····

Seafood Medley: Prepare recipe except use 1 pound fresh white fish fillets, 1 pound shrimp, and 1 pound bay scallops. Cook shrimp and scallops as directed, then heat 2 tablespoons olive oil in a pan and sauté fish fillets for 5 to 6 minutes until done. Let cool and cut into chunks. Refrigerate shrimp and scallops in marinade for 2 to 3 hours. Add fish fillets just before serving.

Making the Marinade

Preparing the Seafood

- In a small nonmetal dish, combine all the marinade ingredients: the juice of 2 to 3 lemons (depending on your taste), extra-virgin olive oil, crushed garlic, chopped parsley, chopped fennel leaves, diced red bell peppers, red wine vinegar, salt, and pepper.

- Mix well, and set aside.

- Wash the squid bodies and tentacles thoroughly in cold water. Cut the bodies into ¼-inch rings, and dice the tentacles. Set aside.

- You can also buy the squid already cleaned at most fish markets.

- Shrimp can be purchased whole—you will have to peel and devein these—or already removed from the shell.

- Both the shrimp and the scallops should be rinsed under cold running water in a colander.

SAUTÉED SCALLOPS

Scallops go well with different sauces, but simply sautéing them is the best way to enjoy their flavor

Italian scallops are very sweet. Once when I was in Italy, I asked a fish vendor the secret to cooking scallops. He just looked at me amused and quickly opened a scallop shell, scooped out the pearl-colored scallop, and popped it into his mouth.

Keep scallops covered and refrigerated. Do not let them rest directly on ice, or they will lose flavor and become watery.

Scallops are always sold out of their shell and by the pound. Bay scallops are small and delicate; on average, thirty-five scallops make up a pound.

Sea scallops are larger (on average, fifteen comprise a pound); while they're not as delicate as bay scallops, they're still very tender. They are also sold frozen. *Yield: serves 4*

Ingredients:

1 pound fresh sea scallops

Salt and ground black pepper

2 tablespoons butter, divided

2 tablespoons dry white vermouth

1 tablespoon finely chopped fresh Italian parsley

Sautéed Scallops

- Rinse the scallops under cold running water to remove any sand or grit, and pat them dry with paper towels. Season lightly with salt and pepper.

- Sauté the scallops in 1 tablespoon of the but-

ter in a frying pan (see technique).

- Add the vermouth to the hot frying pan, swirl in the remaining butter, add the parsley, and pour the sauce over the scallops.

MAKE IT EASY

An easy way to tell the difference between bay and sea scallops is to remember what each is named for. Bay scallops are smaller than sea scallops, just as a bay is smaller than the sea. Both scallops are tender when correctly cooked, but bay scallops are slightly sweeter and more tender. You can substitute either for the other. Beware of calico scallops, an inferior variety sometimes sold as bay scallops.

• • • • RECIPE VARIATION • • • •

Grilled Scallops: Prepare recipe except thread scallops onto metal skewers, or wooden skewers that have been soaked in cool water for 30 minutes. Grill over medium coals or 4 to 7 minutes, until just opaque. Make sauce as directed, place skewers on a serving plate, and pour sauce over all of it. You can also use a grill basket to cook the scallops instead of skewering them.

Sautéing Scallops

- In a frying pan large enough to hold the scallops in one layer, heat half the butter until it begins to turn brown.

- Sauté the scallops for 3 to 5 minutes, turning, until

- they're golden brown on both sides and just firm to the touch.

- Remove to a serving platter, and cover to keep warm.

Making a Butter Sauce

- All butter sauces are made by blending cold butterfat into a reduced acid. In this recipe, the acid is the vermouth.

- After you add the vermouth to the hot pan, allow it to reduce.

- Then whisk in the cold butter. As the butter warms up in the hot pan, it develops a creamy consistency, the basis of a good sauce.

ROASTED GARLIC CRAB

I don't think I've ever made a simpler or more successful dish in my life

Roasted garlic tastes totally different from garlic prepared any other way. Preheat the oven to 350° to 375°F for 5 minutes. Select a whole head of garlic with big cloves, and cut the top off crosswise. Place the head of garlic on a piece of aluminum foil. Drizzle it generously with extra-virgin olive oil, and season with salt and black pepper. Close up the foil all around the seasoned garlic, and place it in the oven to roast for an hour. Let the cooked garlic cool, squeeze the pulp out of each clove, and use it in salads or on bread as a spread.

If you're buying cooked crab meat, be aware that its salt content could be high—salt increases shelf life.
Yield: serves 4

KNACK ITALIAN COOKING

Ingredients:

6 tablespoons (³/₄ stick) unsalted butter

6 tablespoons extra-virgin olive oil

2 tablespoons minced garlic

4 Dungeness crabs, about 1¹/₄ pounds each (ask your supermarket or fish market to remove all the inedible parts)

Salt and freshly ground black pepper

3 tablespoons freshly squeezed lemon juice

¹/₃ cup finely chopped fresh Italian flat-leaf parsley

Roasted Garlic Crab

- Preheat the oven to 500°F.

- Heat the butter, oil, and garlic in a very large ovenproof sauté pan over medium-high heat.

- Rinse the crabs under cool running water. Add the crabs to the pan, season with salt and pepper to taste, and toss well. Transfer the pan to the oven; roast until the garlic turns light brown and the crab is heated through, about 12 minutes. Toss once halfway through.

- Pour the crabs into a large warm serving bowl, add the lemon juice and parsley, and toss well.

···· RECIPE VARIATION ····

Roasted Garlic Crab Legs: Prepare the recipe as directed, but replace the Dungeness crabs with 4 to 5 pounds of king crab legs. The legs will probably be sold frozen; thaw them according to directions from the butcher. Cook the garlic in the butter and olive oil for 3 to 4 minutes before adding the crab legs. Roast the legs for 4 to 6 minutes, until heated through.

Garlic becomes sweet and tender when it's roasted because the compounds that make it taste so strong can no longer react after its cells have been heated. Garlic is very good for you. It contains high amounts of selenium, manganese, vitamin B6, and vitamin C. People who eat garlic every day may have a reduced risk of some diseases, including heart disease and stroke.

Heating the Butter Mixture

- In a very large ovenproof sauté pan, melt the 6 table-spoons of butter.

- Add the 6 tablespoons of oil and blend well.

- Add 2 tablespoons of minced garlic to the sauté pan. Mix well with the butter and olive oil.

- Be very careful not to burn the garlic, for it will have a bitter taste.

Coating the Crab

- You will need a very large ovenproof sauté pan to make this dish.

- If none is available, heat the butter, olive oil, and garlic in a regular sauté pan. Place the crabs in a very large mixing bowl. Pour the

melted butter mixture over the crabs. Season with salt and pepper.

- Toss the crabs well so they become evenly coated with the butter mixture before roasting them in the oven.

CLAMS STEAMED IN WINE

Cooking in wine not only gives food extra flavor but also tenderizes it

There are two major kinds of clams from the East Coast: hard-shell and soft-shell. Hard-shell clams or quahogs have different names depending on their size.

Littlenecks are the smallest. Very tender, they are used for eating raw or for steaming. Cherrystones are of medium size and the most common. They can be eaten raw or steamed, even though they're tougher than littlenecks.

Chowder clams—also called quahogs—are the largest. Tougher, they are mostly chopped up for use in chowders.

Soft-shells clams are sometime called longnecks because of their shape, or steamers because they're usually served steamed in their own broth with melted butter for dipping. These have a soft shell that does not close completely.
Yield: serves 4

KNACK ITALIAN COOKING

Ingredients:

5¹/₂ pounds fresh clams, still in their shells

3 cups dry white wine

1 onion, peeled

3-4 garlic cloves, peeled

1 red peperoncino (or 1 red chile pepper, fresh or dried)

1 bay leaf

Salt and freshly ground pepper

Clams Steamed in Wine

- Rinse the clams (see technique).

- In a huge pot with a tight-fitting lid, bring the wine to a boil with the onion, garlic, peperoncino, bay leaf, salt, and pepper.

- Add the clams, cover, and simmer until the shells open.

- To eat them, pry open each steamed clam. Pull the meat out of the shell. Remove and discard the black membrane that covers the neck of every clam.

- Steamed clams can be dipped into melted butter. Crusty bread is delicious dunked into the clam broth.

···· RECIPE VARIATIONS ····

Mussels Steamed in Wine: Prepare the recipe as directed, except substitute 6 pounds fresh mussels for the clams. If the mussels have beards (thin filaments that stick out of the shell) pull them off. Scrub the mussels and rinse thoroughly. Discard any that are not tightly closed. Cook as directed. Discard any mussels that have not opened after cooking; serve with the broth.

Shrimp Steamed in Wine: Prepare the recipe as directed, except substitute 2 pounds medium or large shrimp still in the shell. If you'd like, cut along the back of the shell and remove the vein before steaming. Cook the shrimp for 3-4 minutes until they turn pink and curl up. Serve with broth for dipping, and offer a bowl to each diner to hold the shells.

Cleaning Clams

Steaming Clams

- Rinse the clams in several changes of cold water. Discard any clams with cracked shells or clam shells that are open.

- If you're using a fresh peperoncino or chile, cut it in half lengthwise, remove the stem, rinse the seeds out, and mince finely.

- If you're using a dried chile, crumble or chop it.

- When the wine and other ingredients come to a boil, add the clams to the pot. Cover and reduce heat to a simmer. Allow the clams to cook for 3 minutes.

- Check the pot, and remove any opened clams with a pair of tongs. Set the steamed clams aside. Cover to keep them warm.

- Repeat this process until about 10 minutes has elapsed. After that, throw out any clam shells that refuse to open. Serve the steamed clams in a big bowl with the cooking broth.

LOBSTER WITH TANGERINE BUTTER

This dish is perfect when you're in a decadent mood

Fish vendors in Italy take the display of seafood very seriously. The variety is spectacular—everything from orange-red spiny lobsters to tiny glistering clams.

Lobsters must be alive when cooked; look for movement of the legs and claws, and curling of the tail. Meat from the tail, legs, and claws is eaten. It is sweet with a distinctive taste. The claw meat is especially good. Live lobsters can be kept packed in moist heavy paper in the refrigerator.

Lobsters are classified by weight:

Chicken: 1 pound

Quarters: 1¼ pound

Selects: 1½–2¼ pounds

Jumbos: over 2½ pounds

This is truly a memorable dish. Serve with a chilled Chardonnay or Chablis.

Yield: serves 6

Ingredients:

4 quarts water

1 tablespoon salt

6 live lobsters, 1¼–1½ pounds each (or use cooked lobster meat)

Chive-Tangerine Butter:

¾ cup (1½ sticks) unsalted butter

½ teaspoon finely grated tangerine zest

3 tablespoons fresh tangerine juice

1 tablespoon Dijon mustard

¼ cup finely snipped fresh chives

Salt and freshly ground pepper

Lobster with Tangerine Butter

- Prepare the lobsters (see technique).

- In a small saucepan, combine the butter, tangerine zest, tangerine juice, mustard, and chives. Season with salt and pepper. Place over medium heat. As soon as the butter melts, remove the sauce from the heat and let it stand at room temperature for 1 hour.

- Reheat the butter until warm, and divide among six small bowls. Serve 1 lobster per person, accompanied with a small bowl of the warm butter.

···· RECIPE VARIATIONS ····

Crab with Chive-Tangerine Butter: Prepare the recipe as directed, substituting Dungeness crabs or king crab legs for the lobster. Steam the whole crabs for 25 to 30 minutes or until they turn bright red. For the crab legs, thaw if frozen, then simmer for 3 to 5 minutes until hot. Make the butter and serve with the crabs.

Lobster Tails with Citrus Butter: Lobster tails are usually available frozen. Thaw them as directed by the butcher or on the package, then simmer in boiling seasoned water for 3 to 5 minutes until the tails curl and turn deep red. Using sharp scissors, cut down the middle of the bottom of each tail to make serving easier. Serve with butter.

Preparing Lobsters

- Approximately 10 to 15 minutes before serving, bring the water to a boil in a very large stockpot.

- Add the salt and lobsters, immersing them completely.

- Boil until the lobsters turn red and are fully cooked, about 10 minutes.

- Using tongs, transfer the lobsters to large dinner plates, and let them cool slightly.

Extracting Lobster Meat

- To make eating the lobster easier, crack the claws with a meat mallet, and cut along the underside of the tail with kitchen scissors.

- Serve the lobster with small forks and/or lobster picks for extracting the meat.

- These tools are found in every store where kitchen utensils are sold.

SCAMPI WITH TOMATO SAUCE

Crabs and shrimp abound along the Sardinian coast

Scampi is the plural of scampo, a specific kind of shrimp not found in the United States but very popular in Italy. In the U.S. the name scampi is used incorrectly for large shrimp broiled with butter and garlic.

All shrimp should smell fresh and sweet. A strong fishy odor is a sign of spoilage. Shrimp come fresh and frozen. Frozen shrimp should be completely frozen when you buy them.

Thaw in the refrigerator. Fresh or thawed shrimp in the shell should be stored on ice. Peeled shrimp must be wrapped in foil before placing on ice, or they will lose flavor and nutrients. Like most shellfish, shrimp will become tough and rubbery if cooked at too high a temperature or for too long.
Yield: serves 3–4

KNACK ITALIAN COOKING

Ingredients:

2 pounds scampi/shrimp

1 onion, diced

1 garlic clove, minced

4–5 tablespoons olive oil

2 bay leaves

1 small peperoncino (or red chile), finely chopped

1 (28-ounce) can plum tomatoes

Salt, to taste

¾ cup dry white wine

1 tablespoon freshly chopped Italian parsley

Scampi with Tomato Sauce

- Prepare the scampi (see technique).

- In a large frying pan, sauté the onion and garlic in olive oil. Add the bay leaves and peperoncino.

- Pour in the plum tomatoes with their juices. Cover and simmer over medium-low heat for 10 to 15 minutes.

- Add the scampi and salt to taste. Pour in the wine, and simmer for 4 minutes with the lid on.

- Arrange the scampi on a plate; pour over some of the cooking juices, and garnish with the parsley.

•••• RECIPE VARIATIONS ••••

Shrimp with Garlic Butter: Prepare the recipe as directed, except increase garlic cloves to 4. Omit the peperoncino and plum tomatoes; add ¼ cup lemon juice and 1 teaspoon finely grated lemon zest. Cook the onion and garlic in olive oil with bay leaves. Add the lemon juice and wine and bring to a simmer. Add the shrimp; simmer, covered, for 3 to 5 minutes until done. Sprinkle with parsley and serve.

Scallops with Tomato Sauce: Prepare the recipe as directed, but substitute 2 pounds bay or sea scallops for the shrimp. Omit the bay leaves; add 2 sprigs of fresh thyme. Cook the scallops in the tomato mixture for 3 to 6 minutes, until they just turn opaque. Increase the parsley to 2 tablespoons and add a tablespoon of minced fresh basil to the dish.

Preparing Shrimp

- To peel shrimp, pull the tiny legs off from the underside of each. This will loosen the delicate shell, which you can pull off with your fingers.

- To devein, use a paring knife to make a shallow cut along the back of the shrimp. Pull out the skinny black vein.

- Cut the scampi in half lengthwise, and wash thoroughly under cold running water.

San Marzano Tomatoes

- Home cooks in the know as well as professional chefs look for San Marzano when they shop for canned tomatoes from Italy.

- This variety of plum tomato is considered to be the best to use when making tomato sauce.

- Grown in the San Marzano area near Naples, this tomato has a thicker flesh and fewer seeds, and its taste is sweeter and less acidic.

- Just look for San Marzano on the can in your supermarket.

EGGPLANT PARMIGIANA

This aromatic dish is a favorite of my family and probably yours as well

Vegetables are always in season somewhere in Italy—the tender spring peas of Veneto; the wonderful, almost sculpted-looking artichokes of Umbria, tender enough to eat raw; and in summer, the noble eggplant and ruby-red tomatoes of Campania.

Cooking affects vegetables in four ways: texture, flavor, color, and nutrients. Most veggies are cooked al dente, but others, including winter squash, eggplant, and celery, are considered cooked when they are soft.

This dish is simple and delicious.

Yield: serves 4

Ingredients:

1 eggplant, about 1 pound

All-purpose flour, as needed

2 eggs, lightly beaten

³/₄ cup dry bread crumbs, seasoned with salt and ground pepper

Vegetable oil, as needed for frying

1 cup spaghetti sauce (homemade or store-bought)

6 ounces fresh mozzarella cheese, cut into thin slices

1 ounce Parmigiano Reggiano cheese, freshly grated

Eggplant Parmigiana

- Prepare the eggplant and fry it (see technique for both).

- Heat the broiler. Place the eggplant slices on a foil-lined baking sheet, and spread with a little tomato sauce. Top each slice with a slice of mozzarella, and sprinkle with grated Parmigiano. Place the pan under the broiler and cook until cheese is melted and lightly browned.

- Pour the remaining tomato sauce into a saucepan, and heat through.

- To serve, divide the tomato sauce among the serving plates, and top with eggplant rounds.

Pesto Eggplant: Prepare the recipe as directed, except spread the eggplant slices with 1 tablespoon basil pesto each instead of tomato sauce after frying. You can make the pesto yourself or purchase it either fresh in the dairy aisle of the supermarket or bottled with the other sauces and Italian food. For a sauce, combine ⅓ cup pesto with ⅓ cup light cream; heat through.

Baked Eggplant Parmigiana: Prepare the recipe as directed, but dip the eggplant in flour, eggs, and crumbs; place on baking sheet. Bake at 400°F for 12 minutes, turning once. Place a thin layer of spaghetti sauce in the bottom of a baking dish and layer the eggplant on top. Sprinkle with cheeses. Bake at 350°F for 25 to 35 minutes until golden brown.

Preparing the Ingredients

- Freshly grate the Parmigiano Reggiano. It will taste fresher and more flavorful than buying something pre-grated.

- Wash the eggplant and cut it into thin slices.

- Place the flour, eggs, and bread crumbs in separate shallow bowls.

- Dredge the eggplant slices in flour, followed by eggs, followed by bread crumbs. Remember to shake off the excess after each step.

Frying the Eggplant

- In a deep skillet, heat about ¼ inch of vegetable oil until very hot but not smoking.

- Add the eggplant slices in batches, and fry until golden brown on both

sides. Do not overcrowd the pan.

- Carefully transfer the cooked eggplant slices to drain on paper towels.

FENNEL WITH PROSCIUTTO
Fennel has a pronounced taste of licorice

Italians are well acquainted with finocchio (fennel), an ancient vegetable that belongs to the celery family. The feathery leaves are added to salads and cooked in soups, while the bulbous white part is eaten raw or braised (cooked slowly in a little liquid). Vegetables should not be overcooked.

Cook as close to serving time as possible and in small quantities. If the vegetable have to be cooked ahead, undercook them, store them in the refrigerator, and reheat when it's time to serve. Cut vegetables uniformly for even cooking. Start with salted, boiling water when boiling vegetables. Cook green vegetables and those with strong flavors uncovered.

To preserve color, cook white and red veggies in water with a sliced lemon. Cook green vegetables in plain water. Do not cook different vegetables at the same time in the same pan. *Yield: serves 4*

Ingredients:

1 medium-size fennel bulb

1 tablespoon olive oil

1 tablespoon butter

2 garlic cloves, chopped

$1/4$ cup diced white onion

Salt and freshly ground black pepper

4 slices prosciutto

6 dried tomatoes, packed in oil, chopped (store-bought is fine)

$1/4$ cup dry white wine

Freshly grated Parmigiano Reggiano cheese, as needed

Fennel with Prosciutto

- Prepare the fennel (see technique).

- Preheat the oven to 350°F.

- In an ovenproof frying pan, heat the olive oil and butter. Add the garlic and sauté until soft. Remove and discard the garlic. Add the onion to the pan, sauté until soft, and add the fennel quarters. Sprinkle with salt and pepper, cover, and cook for 3 minutes.

- Wrap each fennel quarter with a slice of prosciutto and bake (see technique).

- Serve with grated cheese to sprinkle over the top.

194

Preparing Fennel: Fennel has a mild licorice flavor and a crunchy texture. To prepare it, rinse it thoroughly to remove any sandy soil. Cut off the green stems right where the green stalks meet the white bulb. You can save the stalks to use in making stock or sauces. Remove just the outer layer of the core. The entire bulb is edible, weither raw or cooked.

Grilled Fennel: Prepare recipe by cutting and boiling fennel until tender. Remove from liquid; drain; brush with olive oil; sprinkle with salt and pepper. Cut fennel into quarters and wrap with slices of pancetta. Grill over medium-low coals, turning occasionally, until pancetta is crisp and fennel is tender. Place on a serving plate and sprinkle with sun-dried tomatoes and grated cheese.

Preparing the Fennel

- Remove the feathery tops of the fennel, and set aside. Cut off the long stalks, remove the tough outer layer of the bulb, and trim the core. Cut the core into quarters.

- In a large pot, bring 2 quarts of water to a boil. Add 2 teaspoons salt, the

fennel quarters, and the reserved fennel tops.

- Cover and boil until a knife easily pierces the fennel. Do not overcook. The fennel should hold its shape.

- Drain, and discard the fennel tops.

Wrapping the Fennel

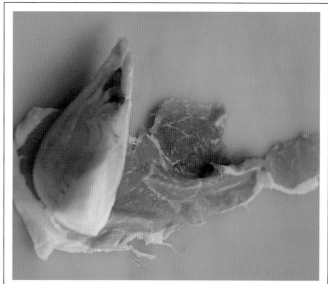

- Remove the fennel from the frying pan to a dish to cool. Set the frying pan aside.

- When the fennel is cool enough to handle, wrap each quarter with a slice of prosciutto.

- Return the fennel quarters to the ovenproof frying pan, sprinkling dried tomatoes atop. Add the wine. Cover the pan with foil, and bake for 20 minutes, or until heated through.

SPICY GRILLED POTATOES

These spiced potatoes are so delicious, everyone will ask for seconds

Potatoes make a great accompaniment to any meat course because they easily absorb the flavors of sauces and meat juices. Red potatoes are often preferred because of their thin skin. They are flavorful and more nutritious than peeled potatoes.

Look for these signs of high-quality potatoes:

• Firm and smooth, dry skin, and no sprouts, a sign of retained extra sugar.

• No green color, a sign that the potato is old and is retaining a substance called solanine, which has a bitter taste.

Keep in a cool dry place (55°F is ideal). Do not refrigerate, because the starch will convert to sugar. *Yield: serves 4*

Ingredients:

1 ½ pounds small new red potatoes, unpeeled and well scrubbed (cut in half if large)

Salt, to taste

1 tablespoon olive oil

1 tablespoon chili powder

3 tablespoons freshly grated Parmigiano Reggiano cheese

1 tablespoon basil pesto (homemade or store-bought)

¼ teaspoon freshly ground black pepper

Spicy Grilled Potatoes

• Light the grill. Fill a large pot three-quarters full with water, and bring to a boil on the stove over high heat.

• Add the potatoes and salt; cook for 10 minutes. Drain in a colander and set aside to cool.

• In a large bowl, combine the oil, chili powder, and potatoes. Place the potatoes on the hot grill, turning occasionally, until browned on all sides.

• In a separate mixing bowl, toss the browned potatoes with the grated cheese, pesto, and fresh pepper.

Cheesy Grilled Potatoes: Prepare the recipe as directed, except cook the potatoes, then grill until crisp and browned. Meanwhile, in a serving bowl combine ⅓ cup grated Parmigiano Reggiano cheese, 1 tablespoon minced fresh thyme leaves, ½ teaspoon salt, ⅛ teaspoon pepper, and ½ cup mascarpone cheese; mix well. Add the hot potatoes and toss until coated; serve immediately.

Grilled Vegetable Skewers: Prepare potatoes and simmer until almost tender. Cut 1 yellow summer squash into 1-inch pieces and clean ½ pound large mushrooms. Thread all vegetables onto soaked wooden skewers. Mix 2 tablespoons oil and 3 tablespoons pesto. Grill skewers, turning and brushing with the pesto mixture, until tender. Sprinkle with ¼ cup grated Parmigiano Reggiano cheese.

Potatoes on the Grill

- Potatoes cook nicely on the grill. With some careful attention, they turn golden brown.

- In this recipe, the potatoes are boiled first, so they will be done in no time on the grill.

- Raw potatoes can also be cooked on the grill, covered with aluminum foil, for 30 to 60 minutes, depending on size. Pierce with a metal skewer to test for doneness.

- Once on the grill, turn the potatoes from time to time, making sure they do not burn.

Coating the Potatoes

- Make sure all the boiled potatoes are coated well with olive oil.

- The chili powder gives these potatoes their spicy flavor.

- The best potatoes for this recipe are red, new, and boiling potatoes.

BROCCOLI W/CAMBOZOLA CHEESE

You could add other vegetables to this dish, like carrots or, in the spring, asparagus

To preserve as much flavor as possible, vegetables should be cooked in plenty of salted boiling water and for as a short a time as possible. A lot of flavors get lost in cooking vegetables, dissolving into the cooking liquid and evaporating. The longer a vegetable cooks, the more flavor it loses.

Salted boiling water is preferred to start vegetables because it shortens the cooking time. Steam vegetables whenever possible.

Add a tablespoon of oil to the cooking water. It will absorb some of the lost flavors and then cling to the vegetables when drained.

Yield: serves 4

Ingredients:

¹/₂ loaf crusty bread

2 tablespoons unsalted butter

Salt and ground black pepper

2 tablespoons extra-virgin olive oil

¹/₂ cup water

1¹/₂ pounds broccoli, florets cut from stems

¹/₄ pound Cambozola cheese (or Gorgonzola)

¹/₂ cup heavy cream

1 teaspoon finely chopped fresh thyme

2 tablespoons pine nuts, toasted

Broccoli with Cambozola Cheese

- Preheat the oven to 375°F. Cook bread in butter in an ovenproof skillet. Season with salt and pepper. Bake for 15 minutes, until browned and crisp outside but still soft inside. Drain and keep warm.

- In a large sauté pan, bring oil, water, salt, and pepper to a boil. Add broccoli, cover, and cook for 5 minutes. Then uncover and sauté until light brown, 5 minutes longer.

- Make cheese sauce. Place bread on warm plates, arrange broccoli atop, and pour sauce over. Sprinkle with pine nuts.

Asparagus with Cambozola Cheese: Prepare the bread and sauce as directed in the recipe. For the asparagus, snap the ends off 1½ pounds fresh asparagus. Rinse well, then place in a large saucepan with olive oil and 2 tablespoons water. Bring to a simmer, then simmer for 4 to 6 minutes until the water evaporates and the asparagus is tender. Place on bread and continue with the recipe.

Mushrooms with Fontina Cheese: Make the bread and cheese sauce as directed, except use ¼ pound grated Fontina cheese in place of the Cambozola cheese. Substitute 1½ pounds cremini or shiitake mushrooms for the broccoli. Trim the ends from the mushrooms and cook in 2 tablespoons olive oil until deep golden brown. Place on bread and proceed with recipe.

VEGETABLES

Sautéing the Pine Nuts

- Pine nuts can be found in the produce department of most supermarkets, usually near the tomatoes.

- Place the pine nuts in a nonstick sauté pan over medium heat.

- Sauté the pine nuts for 1 to 2 minutes, shaking the pan constantly, until they become aromatic.

Making the Cheese Sauce

- In a saucepan, melt the Cambozola over medium heat. Add the heavy cream and mix well.

- Add the thyme, and season well with pepper. Pour this sauce over the broccoli on the browned bread.

- If you can't find Cambozola cheese at the supermarket or in your favorite cheese shop, you can make this recipe with Gorgonzola cheese.

GRILLED PORTOBELLO MUSHROOMS
Portobello mushrooms have a rich flavor and a meaty texture, truly a vegetarian delight

Most types of mushrooms spring up, mature, and vanish within the space of a few days or a couple of weeks, while others appear and disappear within twenty-four hours. Some types favor the same spot; some do not. The unpredictable nature of mushrooms adds to the excitement of the hunt.

One basic fact is that mushrooms reappear at the same

spot and at the same time even after being absent for a few years because its roots persist in a vegetative state in the tree or soil.

The most important rule in mushroom picking is to never eat a wild mushroom unless you are sure of its identity.
Yield: serves 4

Ingredients:

4 large portobello mushrooms

Marinade:

¹/₂ cup olive oil

¹/₂ cup white or red wine vinegar

1 tablespoon low-sodium soy sauce

¹/₂ tablespoon sugar

¹/₄ cup finely chopped fresh parsley (or ¹/₂ tablespoon dried)

¹/₄ cup finely chopped fresh thyme (or ¹/₂ tablespoon dried)

Grilled Portobello Mushrooms

- Separate mushroom stems from caps. Slice each stem in half lengthwise.

- Make the marinade.

- Place mushroom pieces in a shallow dish; pour the marinade over. Let mushrooms marinate for 10 minutes, no longer, turning occasionally

to ensure uniform coating.

- Light the grill (or broiler).

- Remove mushrooms from marinade, and place them over hot grill. Grill on each side for 2 minutes. Remove from the grill, slice, and garnish with herbs.

MAKE IT EASY

Fresh mushrooms are easy to prepare. Most are grown in sterile soil, so they don't need to be washed. Wipe them with a damp cloth and trim off the ends of the stems. Dried mushrooms have to be soaked in boiling-hot water before using. Trim off and discard the stems after the mushrooms have rehydrated, since they are too tough to eat.

• • • • RECIPE VARIATION • • • •

Grilled Mixed Mushrooms: Prepare recipe except substitute 1 pound mixed cremini, shiitake, and button mushrooms for the portobello. Trim off ends; slice large mushrooms, but keep small ones whole. Toss with marinade, let stand for 10 minutes, then drain and place in a grill basket. Grill until tender and browned, about 8 to 10 minutes. Sprinkle with parsley and thyme and serve.

Making the Marinade

- In a small bowl, combine the olive oil, vinegar, soy sauce, sugar, parsley, and thyme.

- Reserve some herbs to garnish the finished dish.

- Blend the marinade well with a whisk for 1 minute.

- Let the marinade sit for 1 hour until the dried herbs soften (this is not necessary if you are using fresh herbs).

Grilling Mushrooms

- Many mushrooms are excellent on the grill. Even common white mushrooms, which can be watery and flavorless, do well on the grill because the heat leaves them firmer and tastier.

- Dried mushrooms should be soaked in warm water for at least 30 minutes before grilling.

- Skewer mushrooms alone or with other food items, and grill them until browned and cooked through.

SAUTÉED ZUCCHINI

Maybe because it won't quit growing once it is planted, many yummy recipes exist for zucchini

Vegetables are an important part of our diet. They supply large amounts of nutrients. They are rich in vitamins C and E. Unfortunately some of these vitamins are lost via long cooking, high temperature, hard water, and oxygen.

Italians have always had a love affair with vegetables, especially zucchini. We pickle it, fry it, stuff it, sauté it—you name it, and we'll do it. The following recipe is a creation I came up with when I was faced with my own abundance of zucchini. It came out so delicious that now my family prefers it over all other vegetables.

Yield: serves 4

Ingredients:

1 pound zucchini

3 tablespoons olive oil

2 garlic cloves, peeled and minced

Salt and freshly ground black pepper

1 tablespoon fresh lemon juice

1 tablespoon balsamic vinegar

Sautéed Zucchini

- Wash the zucchini, trim, and cut into slices. Cut the slices in half if they are large. Or you can cut the zucchini into sticks.

- In a large frying pan, heat the olive oil over medium heat. Add the zucchini, and sauté for a minute or two.

- Add the garlic, and sauté for 5 more minutes, or until the zucchini are tender. Season with salt and pepper. Drizzle with lemon and vinegar.

202

Grilled Zucchini: Prepare the recipe as directed, except after slicing, brush the squash with 2 tablespoons olive oil and sprinkle with salt and pepper. Grill over medium coals for 4 to 7 minutes, turning once, until grill marks appear. Place zucchini on a serving plate. Cook the garlic in the remaining olive oil.

Sautéed Zucchini with Pesto: Prepare the recipe as directed, except omit balsamic vinegar. When the zucchini has been cooked, drizzle with 2–3 tablespoons basil pesto. Sprinkle with 2 tablespoons grated Asiago or Parmigiano Reggiano cheese and serve. You can also let this cool to room temperature and serve it, or chill until cold. Bring to room temperature before serving.

Browning the Zucchini

- If you want to brown your zucchini, you must salt it before cooking. Place the zucchini slices in a colander, and sprinkle with salt. Kosher salt is recommended.

- Salting draws out the excess moisture. Do not add any additional salt to the dish.

- This technique allows the zucchini to sauté, rather than stew in its own juices.

Flavoring with Lemon

- Zucchini is one of many vegetables that come to life with the addition of lemon flavoring.

- Drizzle the cooked zucchini with 1 tablespoon lemon juice. Or sprinkle on 1 teaspoon of grated lemon zest.

- But don't overdo it. A little bit of lemon flavor is all you need.

GORGONZOLA-MUSHROOM SAUCE

The cheese melts easily with cream to create a quick, easy, sauce

According to one legend, an innkeeper from Gorgonzola discovered that his Stracchino cheese had turned blue after a few weeks in his damp, cool cellar. Because he could not afford to lose his profit margin, he decided to sell it anyway. To his eternal gratification, instead of protesting, his customers demanded more of it.

This greenish blue veins of this cheese have a sharp, spicy flavor, contrasting very nicely with the rich, creamy cheese.

Gorgonzola is produced by more than eighty farmhouses, large and small, in the north of Italy. Some still follow the old way of using unpasteurized milk, allowing the curd to become exposed to the mold naturally. Others use pasteurized milk to which the mold is added.

This table cheese is used for pasta, dressings, and salads. *Yield: serves 2*

Ingredients:

2 tablespoons olive oil

2 1/2 cups sliced button mushrooms

1 garlic clove, crushed

1 1/4 cups light cream

6 ounces Gorgonzola cheese, rind removed, crumbled

Salt and ground black pepper

1 pound pasta, cooked

1 tablespoon chopped fresh parsley

1/2 cup chopped walnuts

Gorgonzola-Mushroom Sauce

- Heat the olive oil in a pan over medium heat, and sauté the mushrooms for 5 minutes.

- Add the garlic and cook for 1 to 2 more minutes. Stir in the cream, bring to a boil, and cook for 1 minute. Stir in the Gorgonzola.

- Reheat gently to melt the cheese; do not boil. Season with salt and pepper. Add the sauce to cooked pasta.

- Garnish with chopped parsley and walnuts.

Fontina-Onion Sauce: Prepare the recipe as directed, omitting the mushrooms and Gorgonzola. Cook 2 chopped onions in the olive oil with the garlic until the onions start to turn golden around the edges. Add the cream and boil for 1 minute, then stir in 1½ cups grated Fontina cheese. Finish with pepper, parsley, and ⅓ cup chopped hazelnuts.

ZOOM

Italian Cheeses: There are many types of Italian cheese. Parmigiano-Reggiano, Pecorino, Romano, and Asiago are hard grating cheeses. Fontina, part-skim mozzarella, and provolone cheeses are softer and perfect for melting into sauces. The very soft, uncured cheeses include mascarpone and ricotta. And Gorgonzola is Italy's blue cheese, with veins running through the body of the cheese.

SAUCES

Adding the Cheese

- Remove the rind from the Gorgonzola. Crumble the cheese into a small bowl.

- Into the warm mixture of mushrooms, garlic, and light cream, add the crumbled cheese.

- Stir in the cheese as it melts in the pan over medium heat. Do not allow the sauce to boil.

Combining Sauce and Pasta

- Cook the pasta according to the directions on the package. Drain well, and pour the cooked pasta into a large serving bowl.

- Pour the warm sauce over the hot pasta. Using tongs or a pasta fork, toss the pasta until it is well coated with the sauce.

- A plastic pasta fork does a good job of separating pasta. The teeth in wooden pasta forks eventually loosen up and fall out.

HOMEMADE PESTO

True pesto is made with Italian basil, which has a sweet fragrance

Basil is indispensable to Mediterranean cuisine. From the moment you pull the leaves from the stems, its flavor comes forth.

There are several types of basil. Genoa's variety, which has small leaves and a delicate taste, is best for making pesto. The one from Naples has large leaves and an intense flavor, more suitable for salads and pizza.

Pesto is the ideal no-cook pasta sauce. In Italy, some people still make it by hand with a mortar and pestle, while others prefer using the food processor. I am one of the latter. Use a mixture of Parmigiano Reggiano and Pecorino Romano (half and half). Pine nuts are a great addition, and butter makes it smooth.

Yield: 4 servings

Ingredients:

1 1/2 cups fresh basil leaves, stems removed

2 tablespoons pine nuts

2–3 garlic cloves, roughly chopped

1 teaspoon salt

1 1/2 cups freshly grated Parmigiano Reggiano and Pecorino Romano cheeses, combined

1/2 cup olive oil

2 tablespoons butter, softened

Homemade Pesto

- Put the basil, pine nuts, and garlic in a food processor. Add the salt, and pulse until the mixture forms a chunky paste.

- Add the cheeses, and pulse until smooth. Gradually drizzle in the olive oil, add the butter, and keep pulsing until smooth.

- Store pesto in a screw-top jar in the refrigerator. When you toss it with cooked pasta, thin it slightly, if you like, by adding a little of the hot water used for cooking the pasta.

Spinach Pesto: Prepare the recipe as directed, reducing the amount of basil leaves to 1 cup. Add 1 cup fresh baby spinach leaves to the food processor along with 1 tablespoon freshly squeezed lemon juice. Process the mixture as described in the recipe. Pesto can be frozen; place in hard-sided container, top with a thin layer of olive oil, and freeze for up to 3 months.

Walnut-Arugula Pesto: Prepare the recipe as directed, except substitute 1 cup small arugula leaves for 1 cup of the basil leaves, and replace the pine nuts with ¼ cup chopped toasted walnuts. You can also use other nuts such as hazelnuts, cashews, or pistachios. Other herbs can be used too, like cilantro, sorrel, or parsley.

Using a Food Processor

- The modern-day food processor comes in handy when it's time to make pesto.

- The ingredients are added in stages to the food processor, and you simply pulse the mixture until it has a smooth consistency.

- If a food processor is not available, this can also be done in a blender.

Adding the Olive Oil

- Making pesto is similar to making mayonnaise from scratch. It's essential that you drizzle in the olive oil so that it blends well with all the other ingredients.

- Any good olive oil will do, although extra-virgin olive oil is recommended.

- Store pesto in glass jars with screw-top covers. Always add a thin layer of olive oil to the top of the pesto in the jar. This will prevent the pesto from darkening.

SAUCES

FRESH TOMATO-BASIL SAUCE

This is the simplest of all sauces; it has no equal

September is tomato and basil season. I cannot get enough of either. I use them a lot in salads and sauces, or just eat tomatoes informally as a snack, cut in half with a little salt and a few basil leaves on top. Fresh tomatoes, when in season, are very sweet. However, this sauce—called salsa di pomodori e basilico in Italian—is just as delicious with canned plum tomatoes.

Peel tomatoes by using a swivel blade peeler.

Cut the tomatoes in half; scoop out the seeds, and discard them. Chop the tomato flesh coarsely, and add it to the sauce.

This is the basic sauce I use for anything requiring tomato sauce, including pizza.

Yield: 10 cups

Ingredients:

5 pounds ripe plum tomatoes or 3 (28-ounce) cans crushed plum tomatoes

¹/₂ cup extra-virgin olive oil

¹/₂ cup diced onion

3 garlic cloves, minced

1¹/₂ cups dry red wine

Salt and red pepper flakes, to taste

5 large sprigs basil

Fresh Tomato-Basil Sauce

- Core and puree the tomatoes.

- In a deep heavy pot, heat the olive oil. Add the onion, and sauté until soft. Add the garlic, and sauté until soft. Add the tomatoes; stir to blend.

- Add the wine, salt, red pepper flakes, and basil, stirring well. Bring to a boil, reduce the heat, and simmer for 25 minutes.

- The sauce is ready to be used. It can also be refrigerated for up to a week, or frozen for up to 3 months.

Growing Basil: Fresh basil is essential to Italian cooking, but it can be very expensive to buy it in stores. This herb is easy to grow in the garden in summer, and on a sunny windowsill in winter. Pick the leaves regularly and don't let the plants develop flowers, for all the energy will then go into developing seeds. You can freeze basil leaves whole for longer storage.

···· RECIPE VARIATION ····

Marinara Sauce: Prepare the recipe as directed, except add ½ cup chopped celery and ½ cup chopped carrots to the onion and garlic. Cook until the vegetables are soft. Reduce the wine to ½ cup and omit the basil. Add tomatoes, 1 cup water, and 1 bay leaf. Simmer for 30 to 40 minutes, until thickened. Season to taste with salt and pepper; use immediately or freeze.

Pureeing Fresh Tomatoes

Sautéing Ingredients

SAUCES

- If you're using fresh tomatoes, core them and cut them into coarse chunks.

- Insert the tip of a sharp paring knife about 1 inch into the tomato at an angle all around the core. Use a sawing motion, and turn the tomato until the core is cut free.

- If you like a smooth sauce, puree the tomatoes in a food processor. For a more rustic sauce, use the coarse chunks to make the sauce.

- To sauté means to cook food in very little fat, and it should be done quickly.

- The food should be cut into small uniform pieces or thinly sliced. When the fat is very hot, the food is tossed in and cooked by shaking the pan back and forth with an upward flick of the wrist. This causes the food to jump around in the pan.

- Sauté is derived from the French verb *sauter,* which means "to jump."

RED PEPPER CREAM SAUCE

This sauce made with red bell peppers and cream is a treat for pasta

Peperoni is the Italian term for sweet peppers (not the dried sausage used on pizza). A creamy red pepper sauce is versatile yet feels fancier than your typical everyday red sauce.

When you're planning to roast peppers, shop for those that have a smooth bottom and thick walls. These are the easiest to peel.

Brush the peppers with olive oil, then roast them whole under a broiler, turning occasionally, until all the skin is charred. Place them in a paper bag and close it tightly to let them steam. Peel them, making sure not to lose the juices.

Do not rinse under water, or they will lose flavor. Discard the seeds, and cut the peppers into long strips. Place the strips in a clean bowl; add the juices, 3 tablespoons of extra-virgin olive oil, and salt to taste. Refrigerate, covered, for 2 to 3 days before serving.

Yield: 3 cups

Ingredients:

olive oil to coat

4 red bell peppers

1/4 cup (1/2 stick) butter

2 garlic cloves, minced

1 cup heavy cream or half-and-half

1 teaspoon grated nutmeg

1 1/2 teaspoons salt

1/4 teaspoon freshly grated black pepper

1/4 cup minced fresh basil

Red Pepper Cream Sauce

- Roast the peppers (see technique).

- Puree the roasted peppers (see technique).

- In a large frying pan, heat the butter, and sauté the garlic over medium heat until soft. Add the pepper puree and mix well. Reduce the heat and gradually stir in the heavy cream. Add the nutmeg, salt, and pepper; cook, stirring, for 5 minutes. Remove from the heat, and stir in the basil.

- Serve immediately, or refrigerate for up to 3 days.

Roasted Red Pepper Sauce: Prepare the recipe as directed, omitting the heavy cream. Substitute 1 (14-ounce) can undrained diced tomatoes or 3 chopped red tomatoes; add to sauce with ½ teaspoon dried oregano. Simmer for 7 to 9 minutes until peppers are very soft, then puree the sauce, either with an immersion blender or in a food processor. Season to taste and serve.

Roasted Pepper and Mushroom Sauce: Prepare the peppers as directed, puree, and set aside. Wipe ½ pound button or cremini mushrooms, trim off the stems, and slice ¼ inch thick. Add to the butter with the garlic and 1 small chopped onion; cook until the mushrooms give up their liquid and turn golden brown. Add the pepper puree and ½ cup heavy cream; finish the sauce as described.

Roasting Peppers

- Coat the peppers with olive oil and place them on a lightly greased baking sheet. Broil, turning occasionally, until blackened all over, about 15 minutes.

- Place the peppers in a large paper bag, close the bag tightly, and set aside for 25 minutes to let them steam.

Pureeing Roasted Peppers

- After the roasted peppers have steamed for 25 minutes in a paper bag, remove them from the bag.

- Peel the roasted peppers. The charred skin will come off easily. Remove the seeds and cores.

- Place the peppers in a food processor, and puree until smooth. Set aside.

SAUCES

BUTTER & CREAM SAUCE

This spectacular sauce is usually served with fettuccine or tagliatelle

This wildly popular cream sauce comes to us from Rome, contrary to the popular belief that it is a northern Italian dish. It is named for a restaurant owner, Alfredo, who was said to have given his pasta a final toss with a gold spoon and fork before sending it to the table.

With a few modifications, the recipe can be used for cheese fondue, traditionally seen as both a nourishing meal and a sensible way to use leftovers. Cheese fondue has always been a favorite in the Alps. Their version calls for a mixture of Emmental and Greyerzer cheese melted together with white wine, herbs, and a little lemon juice. Other versions call for egg yolks.

Yield: serves 3–4

Ingredients:

3 tablespoons butter

1 cup heavy cream

Pinch freshly ground nutmeg

Salt and freshly ground black pepper

$1/2$–1 cup grated Parmigiano Reggiano cheese

1 pound cooked pasta (fettuccine is recommended)

Butter and Cream Sauce

- In a large skillet over medium-high heat, combine the butter and cream. Bring to a boil, stirring frequently until the cream has reduced almost by half.

- Add the nutmeg, salt, and a generous amount of black pepper. Remove from the heat.

- Add the freshly grated cheese to the skillet, then add the cooked pasta, tossing well to coat with sauce. Season to taste with more salt and pepper.

212

RECIPE VARIATION

Cheese Fondue: Prepare the recipe as directed, except double the butter and cream amounts. Cook the cream in the butter until it is reduced. Add 1 cup grated Fontina cheese, ½ cup grated Gruyère, ½ cup shredded Parmigiano Reggiano, nutmeg, salt, and pepper. Stir over very low heat until the cheeses melt. Serve with cubes of bread for dipping.

Making the Sauce

- Timing is everything with this dish.

- As the water for the pasta comes to a boil, start making the sauce by melting the butter in a large skillet.

- Add the cream, and salt the pasta water. Cook the pasta as the sauce reduces. Add the remaining ingredients to the sauce.

Coating the Pasta

- To cook the pasta: Bring 4 quarts of water to a boil in a large pot.

- Add a tablespoon of salt and the pasta to the boiling water, stirring well. When the pasta is al dente, drain it well.

- Add the cooked pasta to the skillet, using tongs or a pasta fork to turn the pasta until it is well coated with the sauce.

CALABRESE MEAT SAUCE

This sauce is truly a comfort food for winter, summer, and in-between days

One of the best combinations of meat for tomato sauce is pork and beef. When I was young the scrumptious smell of this dish would reach our neighbors rapidly, prompting them to comment, much to my mother's pleasure.

Calabria is the Italian region located on the toe of southern Italy, and it is where I came from. This is the ragu sauce I grew up with, and it has been passed through the generations. It is the one we made every Sunday and on special occasions. This sauce starts with a *soffritto*—sautéed aromatic vegetables—to which the remaining ingredients are added. It is a hearty sauce that is perfect over chunky types of pasta, as well as slices of polenta. *Yield: 8 cups*

Ingredients:

2 tablespoons olive oil

2 garlic cloves, chopped

1 medium-size onion, coarsely chopped

1 celery rib, coarsely chopped

1 large carrot, coarsely chopped

1 pound beef round or chuck steak, cut into $^1/_2$-inch cubes

1 pound pork tenderloin, cut into $^1/_2$-inch cubes

$^1/_2$ cup red dry wine

3 (28-ounce) cans plum tomatoes

1 bay leaf

1 tablespoon salt

Calabrese Meat Sauce

- Make the soffritto and brown the meat (see technique).

- Add the tomatoes, bay leaf, and salt (see technique).

- Simmer the ragu, covered, over low heat until the meat is tender, about 45 minutes. Remove and discard the bay leaf.

- Use immediately, or freeze for up to 3 months.

Slow-Cooker Ragu: Use ingredients called for, but layer garlic, onion, celery, and carrot in a 4-quart slow cooker. Cook meat cubes in olive oil until browned; place on top of vegetables. Add the wine and tomatoes to the saucepan; boil for 10 minutes, scraping up the brown bits, then pour into a slow cooker. Add the bay leaf and salt. Cover and cook on low for 8 to 10 hours until the sauce is blended.

Ragu Bolognese: Prepare recipe except start with ⅓ cup chopped pancetta. Brown pancetta in olive oil, then remove to drain. Add garlic, onion, celery, and carrot; cook until tender. Substitute 1 pound ground beef, 1 pound ground pork, and ½ pound ground veal for cubed meat. When sauce is done, stir in ¼ cup light cream and blend.

Browning the Meat

Adding the Tomatoes

- Make the soffritto: In a large saucepan, heat the oil. Add the garlic, and sauté until soft. Add the onion, celery, and carrot; sauté for 5 to 7 minutes, or until soft.

- Using a slotted spoon, remove the vegetables from the pan. Set aside.

- Pat the meat dry with paper towels; add to the pan in which the soffritto was cooked, and brown it well.

- After making the soffritto and browning the meat, add the wine, and simmer for 5 minutes.

- Add the tomatoes, bay leaf, and salt. Return the vegetables to the pan.

- Simmer the ragu, covered, over low heat until the meat is tender, about 45 minutes.

PRESNITZ

These melt-in-the-mouth buttery pastry whirls are filled with fruits and nuts

Friuli is far away from the usual tourist track that runs through Italy. The visitors who do reach this Alpine region, bordering the former Yugoslavia, choose it for its unspoiled natural beauty, excellent cuisine, and famous wines. This is where prosciutto di San Daniele is made. Its dishes mingle Austrian, Hungarian, Slovenian, and Croatian influences, and so does

the name presnitz. A meal there might conclude with a slice of the traditional presnitz made of pastry whirls filled with walnuts, hazelnut, almonds, pine nuts, and raisins soaked in rum.

Yield: serves 8

Ingredients:

Pastry:

2 cups all-purpose flour, divided

1 cup butter

5–6 tablespoons milk

Juice of 1 lemon

1 egg

Salt

Flour, as needed for work surface

Filling:

²/₃ cup chopped walnuts

²/₃ cup chopped hazelnuts

²/₃ cup chopped almonds

²/₃ cup pine nuts

²/₃ cup raisins, soaked in rum

²/₃ cup candied fruit (your choice)

Butter, as needed for greasing pans

1 egg, beaten

Powdered sugar, as needed

Presnitz

- Mix half the flour with butter in a bowl, cover, and set aside overnight. The next day, combine remaining flour, milk, lemon juice, egg, and salt in another bowl. Set aside for 1 hour. Knead the two mixtures together; roll thinly into a rectangle on a floured cloth.

- Scatter nuts and fruit atop. Roll into a sausage shape; slice it into rounds.

- Preheat oven to 400°F. Butter a baking dish; lay slices side by side to fill it. Brush with beaten egg; bake for 40 minutes.

- Dust with powdered sugar.

Dried Fruit Croissants: Prepare the recipe as directed, except use ⅔ cup each dried currants, golden raisins, rum-soaked raisins, dried cherries, and dried cranberries in place of the nuts. You can soak all of the fruit in rum or dry red wine for 1 to 2 hours before using. Drain the fruit well before layering it on the dough. Sprinkle 1 teaspoon lemon zest over the fruit before rolling up the croissants.

Vanilla Glaze: Drizzle the finished croissants with a glaze for a nice touch. In small bowl, combine 1 cup powdered sugar with 2–3 tablespoons light cream, ½ teaspoon vanilla, and 1 tablespoon melted butter; blend well. Drizzle this mixture over the cooled croissants. You can flavor this glaze with 1 tablespoon lemon juice instead of the vanilla, or add 2 tablespoons cocoa powder for a chocolate glaze.

Chopping Nuts

- If your knife skills are good, you can chop nuts on a cutting board with a very sharp chef's knife.

- You can also chop nuts with a special nut grinder, a blender, or a food processor.

- It is important that you exercise caution with these tools. Operate in short spurts so the nuts end up chopped, not finely ground.

Soaking Raisins in Rum

- In a bowl, soak the raisins in enough rum to cover them. You can use either light or dark rum. Set aside for 30 minutes.

- Drain off the rum, and add the raisins to a bowl containing the candied fruit of your choice.

DESSERTS

217

ESPRESSO GELATO

Espresso is the favorite coffee of Italians and is drunk from morning to evening

We Italians love espresso so much we invent new recipes to incorporate it. This is a classic example.

In Italy espresso is just called *caffe*. It is drunk throughout the day; people even drink it late in the evening as a digestive after a sumptuous meal. Real espresso should be drunk very hot in a cup that has been warmed, and usually with a lot of sugar. The delicate crema—the light brown foam layer that floats on top of the dark espresso—is a sign that the espresso machine is working at the correct temperature and pressure and produces a perfect espresso.

The difference between gelato and ice cream is the percentage of fat. Gelato has very little. *Yield: serves 6*

Ingredients:

8³/₄ ounces egg yolks (about 10–12)

1 cup sugar

¹/₂ cup espresso

Espresso Gelato

- In a large bowl, mix all the ingredients together using a very big whisk. Chill for 30 minutes.

- Pour the mixture into a container, and leave it in the freezer until frozen.

- Alternatively, chill for 30 minutes, then place in the freezer for 2 hours, stirring thoroughly with a large whisk every 10 to 15 minutes or so. Place in the freezer until frozen.

Chocolate Gelato: Prepare the recipe as directed, except instead of espresso, melt 3 squares semisweet chocolate in ¼ cup freshly brewed coffee. Add to the egg yolk and sugar mixture and place in a double boiler. Cook over simmering water for 10 to 14 minutes until thickened. Cool completely, then chill until cold and freeze according to directions.

ZOOM

You can use an ice cream or gelato maker to freeze this mixture. Most of the newer types have a removable center container you freeze for 4 to 6 hours. Then just pour the gelato mixture into the container, place it in the machine, and turn it on. When the mixture is frozen, decant the gelato into a freezer container and let it ripen in the freezer for 3 to 4 hours.

Three Simple Ingredients

- It's pretty amazing that something as wonderful as gelato is made simply with egg yolks, sugar, and espresso.

- Back in the seventeenth century, Francesco Procopio dei Coltelli from Sicily was the first to make what is now called gelato.

- Today the best ice cream in Italy is made by local gelaterie, shops that sell ice cream much fresher than the commercially made variety.

Using a Balloon Whisk

- The best way to make gelato is with a very large whisk, which is known as a balloon whisk.

- The more loops of flexible wire a balloon whisk has, the better job it will do.

- Whipping is a technique that incorporates air into ingredients. A large balloon whisk draws in more air than a regular balloon whisk.

DESSERTS

TIRAMI SU

Cognac, Marsala, Amaretto, whiskey, rum, and coffee liqueur can be added to this creamy, cold dessert

Mascarpone is a creamy, soft cheese with a delicate flavor. With a fat content of 50 percent, it is mostly used for desserts. It is produced by using the cream of cow's milk, and lemon juice or white vinegar is added to start the coagulation.

Tirami su—the term literally means "pick me up"—is enjoyed as a dessert throughout Italy. Many regions claim to have invented it. The natives of Piedmont point to their sponge cake (ladyfingers). Lombardians argue that mascarpone originated in their region, thus the honors should go to them. Venetians and Tuscans are just as eager to take credit for its invention, and the Romans regard the dessert as typically Italian and, therefore, Roman in origin. *Yield: serves 8*

Ingredients:

³/₄ cup heavy cream

5 tablespoons sugar, divided

4 egg yolks

1 pound mascarpone cheese

24 ladyfingers

¹/₄ cup strong espresso coffee

¹/₄ cup Amaretto

Cocoa powder, as needed

Tirami Su

- In a bowl, whip the cream with 1 tablespoon sugar until stiff.

- In another bowl, whisk the egg yolks with the remaining sugar until creamy, using a handheld mixer on high. Stir in the mascarpone one spoonful at a time and then, at a lower speed, stir in the whipped cream.

- Construct the tirami su (see technique).

- Sprinkle with the espresso and Amaretto mixture, and spread the remaining cream on top. Sprinkle with cocoa powder, and chill for at least 1 hour in the refrigerator.

Use Other Liqueurs: You can substitute any Italian or French liqueur for the Amaretto in this recipe. Think about using Marsala wine, cognac, a good smooth aged whiskey, or rum. Any of your favorite liqueurs would be delicious. The liqueur is mixed with the espresso to soak the ladyfingers so each bite has a rich taste and to help make the dry cookies moist.

Chocolate Tirami Su: Prepare the recipe as directed, except melt 3 1-ounce squares of semisweet chocolate in a small saucepan; cool for 15 minutes. Beat into the egg yolk mixture along with ¼ cup powdered sugar. When the tirami su is completed, shave semisweet or bittersweet chocolate over the finished dessert; chill and serve as directed.

Whipping Heavy Cream

- In a bowl, whip the cream with 1 tablespoon of sugar until stiff.

- When cream is whipped, it not only grows in volume, but also becomes stiff.

- Be careful not to overdo this whipping. The ideal stage is when the texture is smooth, and the cream is thick enough to stand with droopy peaks when dropped from a spoon.

Construct the Tirami Su

- Line a deep oblong dish with half of the ladyfingers.

- In a bowl, combine the espresso and Amaretto; sprinkle over the ladyfingers, making sure not to soak them.

- Spread a layer of cream on top, and cover with another layer of ladyfingers.

DESSERTS

STUFFED DRIED FIGS
These are a perfect holiday treat

Fichi secchi ripieni is the dessert that I would wait anxiously for every Christmas season. My grandmother and my mother would make a ton of these delicious little mouthfuls, enough to last us for the holidays and the winter.

At the end of the day, we would gather around the *focolare* (a fireplace that was both our main source of heat and the stove we used for dishes that required slow cooking). There we would munch on delicious stuffed figs while my grandmother would entertain us with stories of her youth.

Yield: serves 2

Ingredients:

2 ounces hazelnuts, toasted, with skins removed

2 ounces almonds, blanched, with skins removed

Grated rind of 2 lemons

8 large dried figs

Honey, as needed

Stuffed Dried Figs

- Chop the toasted hazelnuts and blanched almonds.

- In a bowl, mix together the hazelnuts, almonds, and lemon rind.

- Make a cut in the middle of each fig, and put some of the mixture in each.

- Place the stuffed figs on a greased baking sheet, drizzle them with honey, and bake in a preheated 350°F oven for about 10 minutes.

Stuffed Dates: Prepare the recipe as directed, except substitute 8 large fresh pitted dates for the dried figs. Do not bake the dates. The best dates to use are called Medjool. These dates are large and rich and have a wonderful caramel flavor. You can also use different nuts in the filling. A combination of pistachios and hazelnuts, or almonds and pine nuts, would be delicious stuffed into dates or figs.

Mascarpone-Stuffed Figs: Prepare the recipe as directed, but use the following stuffing: Combine ½ cup mascarpone cheese with ¼ cup chopped dried cherries and ¼ cup miniature semisweet chocolate chips. Add 1 teaspoon grated lemon rind and 2 tablespoons finely chopped toasted hazelnuts. Place the figs in a baking dish, drizzle with honey, and bake as directed.

Grating the Lemon Rind

- Wash and dry a lemon. Cut away any lettering that is stamped on the rind.

- Rub the fruit lightly over the rough surface of a grater or rasp.

- You want to remove only the colored portion of the rind. Do not grate the white portion of the rind, which is bitter.

- This technique can also be used to grate an orange.

Stuffing the Figs

- With a very sharp paring knife, make a cut in the middle of each dried fig. Be careful not to pierce the fig all the way through.

- Divide the stuffing mixture equally among the 8 dried figs.

- Push the stuffing mixture into the cut. Place the stuffed figs on a greased baking sheet.

DESSERTS

CANNOLI & ESPRESSO

Caffe ristretto: double strength and sharp

Cannoli (plural of cannolo) are fried pastry rolls with a delicious filling made with sweet ricotta, chocolate, and candied fruits. These were once a special treat at Carnival time in Italy. Enjoyed now year-round, cannoli come to us from Sicily. They are usually served with espresso.

Caffe con panna: A diluted espresso with a topping of unsweeted whipped cream and a dusting of cocoa on top.

Caffe shakerato: A popular summer drink throughout Italy, shaken with sugar and ice cubes.

Caffe doppio: A double espresso served in a bigger cup.

Caffe lungo: To make *caffe lungo*, let hot water run through the filter a few seconds longer than usual.

Yield: serves 16

Ingredients:

5 tablespoons butter

7 tablespoons sugar

3 eggs, divided

3¹/₂ tablespoons dry white wine

1 teaspoon vanilla essence or extract

1 pinch salt

5 ounces all-purpose flour

Vegetable oil, as needed for frying

Powdered sugar, as needed

Filling:

1 pound fresh ricotta

¹/₂ cup sugar

1 teaspoon vanilla essence or extract

2 tablespoons orange flower water (if available)

2 tablespoons mixed candied orange and lemon peel, finely chopped

1¹/₂ tablespoons angelica, finely chopped (if available)

10 glacé cherries (candied cherries in a jar), finely chopped

3 ounces dark chocolate, finely chopped

Cannoli

- Cream butter and sugar. Mix in 2 eggs, wine, vanilla, and salt. Gradually add flour; knead dough 10 minutes until elastic. Cover; cool 2 hours.

- Roll dough to ¹/₁₆ inch thick; cut into 16 (5-inch) squares. Lay a cannoli tube over each square to make shells.

- Heat oil in a saucepan. Place 3 or 4 cannoli side by side; fry until golden, 1½ to 2 minutes. Drain. Once cool, remove tubes.

- Make filling. Fill cannoli using an espresso spoon or pastry bag; arrange on a plate, sprinkle with powdered sugar.

Deep-Frying Cautions: Take care when deep-frying and you will have success. A thermometer is helpful. Most foods are deep-fried at 350° to 375°F. If you don't have a thermometer, drop a cube of bread into the oil; it should brown in about 60 seconds. Don't overcrowd the pan or the oil temperature will drop too low and the food will be soggy. Use tongs and stand well back when adding food to hot oil.

Chocolate Cannoli: Make cannoli shells as directed; drain on paper towels and cool completely. For the filling, beat the ricotta with the sugar. Beat in ⅓ cup cocoa powder along with ½ cup powdered sugar and 1 teaspoon vanilla until smooth. Fold in the chopped dark chocolate and fill the cooled shells. Sprinkle with powdered sugar through a small sieve and serve.

Using Cannoli Tubes

The Right Consistency

- Tubes especially designed for making cannoli can be purchased in restaurant supply stores, stores that specialize in baking supplies, and high-end gourmet shops.

- These tubes can be made of metal or bamboo. They are

6 inches long and ¾ inch in diameter.

- Beat the remaining egg in a small bowl. Lay a tube diagonally across each square. Brush the corners with beaten egg, and fold the two opposite corners over the tube.

- The filling for cannoli should have a creamy consistency. To achieve that, the ricotta must be drained.

- Place the ricotta in a fine sieve, or wrap it in cheesecloth, and set it over an empty bowl. Allow it to drain for 45 minutes.

- In a bowl, combine the drained ricotta with the sugar, vanilla, and orange flower water. Mix in the candied orange and lemon peel, angelica, glacé cherries, and chocolate. Mix well until smooth.

MERINGUES (SCIUMETTE)
This light, simple dessert is an Italian favorite

When it comes to finding something sweet with which to end a meal, Ligurians do not rely on complicated desserts. They much prefer little cakes and pastries, such as sciumette ("floating islands," or meringues) and espresso. The following types of espresso are some of the most popular in Italy:

Caffe e latte: Equal parts coffee and hot milk.

Caffe corretto: Coffee served with an alcoholic beverage either in it or alongside it. In the north, grappa is prominent, while Italians in the the central and southern regions prefer anisette liqueur.

Cappuccino: This was so named because of its color—the result of the mixture of espresso and frothy milk—was believed to resemble the habits of the Capuchin monks.
Yield: serves 5

Ingredients:

4 eggs, separated

¹/₂ cup superfine sugar, divided

4 cups milk

1 tablespoon all-purpose flour

¹/₂ tablespoon fresh pistachios, shelled and crushed

Powdered cinnamon, as needed

Sciumette

- Make "snowballs." Remove the milk from heat, add remaining sugar, stir in flour, and set aside to cool.

- Cook pistachios for a few minutes in a little milk; drain. Beat egg yolks, and gradually add to milk and flour mixture. Add pistachio puree.

- Put mixture back on heat in a hot bain-marie.

- Allow to thicken a little over low heat, making sure water doesn't boil. Pour thickened mixture into a bowl, decorate with "snowballs," and sprinkle with cinnamon.

Lemon Floating Island: Prepare recipe, omitting the pistachios. Add 1 tablespoon of lemon juice to the whites while beating them; cook as directed. Use 3½ cups milk to make sauce; add ⅓ cup lemon juice and cook until thick. Omit pistachio puree. Add 2 teaspoons finely grated lemon zest to sauce. Place poached meringues in the sauce and sprinkle with finely chopped toasted hazelnuts.

Espresso Floating Island: Prepare the recipe as directed, except add 1 teaspoon espresso powder to the egg whites along with the sugar; beat until stiff. Omit 1 cup milk; add 1 cup strong brewed coffee in its place. Cook the meringues as directed, then make the sauce, omitting the pistachio puree, and thicken as directed. Sprinkle with cinnamon.

Making Snowballs

- In a bowl, beat the egg whites with 1 tablespoon of the sugar until stiff.

- In a casserole, bring the milk to a boil. Using a spoon, very gently add the beaten egg whites, which should set immediately.

- Cook the resulting "snowballs" very briefly. Lift them up with a slotted spoon to drain in a sieve.

Using a Bain-Marie

- Bain-marie is a French term for a cooking technique that calls for a water bath.

- Place a container of food into a large shallow pan of warm to hot water, which surrounds the food with gentle moist heat.

- The bain-marie is then placed on top of the stove or in the oven to cook.

- This technique is used to make custards, sauces, and mousses.

DESSERTS

WINE PAIRINGS
White and red wines to go with your food

A selected glass of wine enhances the taste of food. As a general rule, white, rosé, and sweet dessert wines should be served at colder temperature than red wines. Keep in mind, however, if they are served too cold they will loose some balance in taste. On the other hand, cold temperatures in red wines—particularly heavy reds—increase the bitterness that is already present.

When it comes to choosing a certain wine, the rule of thumb, according to me, is: drink what you like. However, if you like to enhance the taste of both food and wine when paired together, this rule of thumb might be more fitting: Do not serve a strong wine with a delicate meal and vice versa.

This means that you do not have to worry about only choosing white wines for fish and only choosing red wines for red meat, for example. You can serve a robust white wine with high level of alcohol, such as Greco, with meats and a medium-bodied red wine, such as Barbera (a not-too-rich dry wine), with fish.

The following is a list of various wines that I use with my meals:

White Wines

Dry sparkling wine that is very good with lightly salty foods like olive and onions or nuts:
Prosecco

White wine with lower alcohol levels that are clean and refreshing and pair well with fish, by itself, or with any other kind of summer foods:
Arneis
Pinot Blanc
Pinot Grigio
Tocai
Trebbiano

White wine with low alcohol and a hint of sweetness that is perfect with fish, by itself, or meats like veal:
Muscat
Medium-bodied white wine with medium alcohol level that go well with veal, basic risotto, or risotto with fruit:
Chardonnay
Frascati
Gavi
Orvieto
Vernaccia

Big, bold, robust, dry white wine with high levels of alcohol and that will taste great with red meats and strong flavor foods:
Greco

Rosé Wines

Dry rosé wine:

Grigolino

Red Wines

Simple, dry, fruity wine that pairs well with desserts and light flavor foods or by itself:
Barbera
Corvina
Dolcetto
Merlot
Sangiovese/blend (Italy)
Sangiovese/blend (USA)

Medium rich dry wine that can be served with lamb and pork chops:
Barbera
Corvina
Dolcetto
Nebbiolo

Very rich dry red wine that is dependable with strong flavored foods, such as pizza, steak, or meat balls:
Nebbiolo
Sagiovese/blend

Dessert Wines

Sweet wine that is best-served with desserts, espresso, and fruit:
Muscat
Vin Santo

FIND INGREDIENTS
There are many resources for ingredients other than the grocery store

Catalogs and Online Sources

Amazon Grocery

www.agrocerydelivery.com/

- Amazon.com has a grocery delivery service. Offers general foods and hard to find items.

The Baker's Catalog

- From King Arthur's Flour, this catalog offers cooking equipment and baking ingredients, including specialty flours and flavorings.

Peapod

www.peapod.com

- Online grocery store serving some areas of the United States.

Safeway.com

- Grocery chain offers delivery of food items, as well as recipes and tips for healthy living.

Schwans

- Home delivery service for groceries, serving parts of the United States.

Farmers' markets

Farmers' Markets

www.farmersmarket.com

- Los Angeles Farmers' Market Web site; the original farmers' market.

National Directory of Farmer's Markets

http://farmersmarket.com/

- Site has index of U.S. farmers' markets listed by state.

Farmer's Market Search

http://apps.ams.usda.gov/FarmersMarkets/

- USDA site lets you search for a farmers' market by state, city, county, and zip code, as well as methods of payment.

231

METRIC CONVERSION TABLES

Approximate U.S. Metric Equivalents

Liquid Ingredients

U.S. MEASURES	METRIC	U.S. MEASURES	METRIC
¼ TSP.	1.23 ML	2 TBSPS.	29.57 ML
½ TSP.	2.36 ML	3 TBSPS.	44.36 ML
¾ TSP.	3.70 ML	¼ CUP	59.15 ML
1 TSP.	4.93 ML	½ CUP	118.30 ML
1¼ TSPS.	6.16 ML	1 CUP	236.59 ML
1½ TSPS.	7.39 ML	2 CUPS OR 1 PT.	473.18 ML
1¾ TSPS.	8.63 ML	3 CUPS	709.77 ML
2 TSPS.	9.86 ML	4 CUPS OR 1 QT.	946.36 ML
1 TBSP.	14.79 ML	4 QTS. OR 1 GAL.	3.79 L

Dry Ingredients

U.S. MEASURES	METRIC	U.S. MEASURES		METRIC
1/16 OZ.	2 (1.8) G	2⅘ OZ.		80 G
⅛ OZ.	3½ (3.5) G	3 OZ.		85 (84.9) G
¼ OZ.	7 (7.1) G	3½ OZ.		100 G
½ OZ.	15 (14.2) G	4 OZ.		115 (113.2) G
¾ OZ.	21 (21.3) G	4½ OZ.		125 G
⅞ OZ.	25 G	5¼ OZ.		150 G
1 OZ.	30 (28.3) G	8⅞ OZ.		250 G
1¾ OZ.	50 G	16 OZ.	1 LB.	454 G
2 OZ.	60 (56.6) G	17⅗ OZ.	1 LIVRE	500 G

PRINT RESOURCES & WEB SITES

Where to look for additional information on Italian cooking

There are numerous Web sites, magazines, and other print resources out there that all focus on everything Italian-related. While this is no means a comprehensive list of those resources, here are a few of our favorites for you.

Magazines

Italian Cooking & Living
Bimonthly magazine from the UK that focuses on no-fuss authentic dishes

La Cucina Italiana
Authentic Italian cooking and recipes
www.lacucinaitalianamagazine.com

Tastes of Italia
Celebrity recipes and easy-to-make menus along with tours of Italy, and a focus on Italian culture, travel, and wine
www.inlandempiremagazine.com

Web sites

Barilla
Emphasis on Barilla recipes and ingredients with a special section on nutrition
www.barillaus.com

Chef Maria
The author's personal Web site with emphasis on healthy cooking and fresh recipes
www.chefmaria.com

Ciao Italia
A focus on all-things Italian
www.ciaoitalia.com

Giada DeLaurentiis
The acclaimed Italian chef, TV personality, and author
www.giadadelaurentiis.com

The Italian Chef
Homemade recipes and a focus on travel; blog updated regularly
www.italianchef.com

GLOSSARY
Learn the language first

Al dente: Italian phrase meaning "to the tooth"; describes doneness of pasta.

Alla Bolognese: Means in the style of Bologna, and usually refers to a slow-cooked meat sauce with vegetables and tomato.

Alla Caprese: In the style of Capri, meaning made with tomato, basil, olive oil, and mozzarella cheese.

Bread: To coat with crumbs or crushed crackers before baking or frying.

Broil: To cook food close to the heat source, quickly. Used in slow cooking to add color and flavor.

Brown: Cooking step that caramelizes food and adds color and flavor before cooking in the slow cooker.

Bruschetta: Toasts, usually served with a topping of some sort as an antipasto.

Carpaccio: A dish of raw beef sliced very thin, often seasoned with lemon and olive oil or mayonnaise, served as a salad or antipasto.

Coat: To cover food in another ingredient, as to coat chicken breasts with breadcrumbs.

Chop: To cut food into small pieces, using a chef's knife or a food processor.

Crostini: Toasted bread like a crouton, usually served with a topping of some sort, or sometimes just a drizzle of good olive oil.

Deglaze: To add a liquid to a pan used to sauté meats; this removes drippings and brown bits to create a sauce.

Dice: To cut food into small, even portions, usually about ¼ inch square.

Fold: Combine two soft or liquid mixtures together, using an over-and-under method of mixing.

Grate: To use a grater or microplane to remove small pieces or shreds of food.

Grill: To cook over coals or charcoal, or over high heat.

Herbs: The edible leaves of certain plants that add flavor to food, including basil, marjoram, thyme, oregano, and mint.

Knead: To work dough by mixing, stretching, pressing, and pulling it.

Marinate: To let meats or vegetables stand in a mixture of an acid and oil, to add flavor and tenderize.

Mascarpone: A fresh Italian cream cheese with a very soft, creamy texture and buttery flavor.

Melt: To turn a solid into a liquid by the addition of heat.

Pan-Fry: To cook quickly in a shallow pan, in a small amount of fat over relatively high heat.

Peperoncino: A hot chili pepper used in Italian cuisine.

Porcini: A meaty mushroom used both fresh and dried in Italian cuisine.

Sauté: To cook a food briefly in oil over medium-high heat, while stirring it so it cooks evenly.

Seasoning: To add herbs, spices, citrus juices and zest, and peppers to food to increase flavor.

Simmer: A state of liquid cooking, where the liquid is just below boil.

Spices: The edible dried fruits, bark, and seeds of plants, used to add flavor to food.

Steam: To cook food by immersing it in steam. Food is set over boiling liquid.

Toss: To combine food using two spoons or a spoon and a fork until mixed.

Whisk: Both a tool, which is made of loops of steel, and a method, which combines food until smooth.

INDEX

INDEX

INDEX